Pastoral Essays in Honor of
LAWRENCE BOADT, CSP

READING THE OLD TESTAMENT

EDITED BY
Corrine L. Carvalho

PAULIST PRESS
New York / Mahwah, NJ

Cover and book design by Lynn Else

Parts of the section written by Thomas McCreesh dealing with the proverbs in chapters 10–29 were published in an earlier and shorter form that also included Sirach. They appeared in "Friends and Family in the Wisdom Literature," *The Bible Today* (May/June 2011): 149–55. Printed with permission by Liturgical Press.

Library of Congress Cataloging-in-Publication Data

Pastoral essays in honor of Lawrence Boadt, CSP : reading the Old Testament / Corrine L. Carvalho (editor).
    pages cm
Includes bibliographical references and index.
ISBN 978-0-8091-4838-7 (alk. paper) — ISBN 978-1-58768-250-6
    1. Bible. Old Testament—Criticism, interpretation, etc. I. Boadt, Lawrence. II. Carvalho, Corrine L., editor of compilation.
    BS1171.3.P37 2013
    221.6—dc23

                                                                2013016484

ISBN: 978-0-8091-4838-7 (paperback)
ISBN: 978-1-58768-250-6 (e-book)

Published by Paulist Press
997 Macarthur Boulevard
Mahwah, New Jersey 07430

www.paulistpress.com

Printed and bound in the
United States of America

TABLE OF CONTENTS

CONTRIBUTORS

Corrine L. Carvalho is Professor of Old Testament at the University of St. Thomas in St. Paul, Minnesota, teaching undergraduate students for sixteen years. She holds a graduate degree from Yale University. Her latest book is *Ezekiel, Daniel*, co-authored with Paul Niskanen in the New Collegeville Bible Commentary Series. She is an occasional contributor to both *The Bible Today* and *Give Us This Day*, and frequently gives classes on biblical texts at local churches.

Christopher Frechette, SJ, is Assistant Professor of Old Testament at the Boston College School of Theology and Ministry. He holds a Licentiate in Sacred Theology from the Weston Jesuit School of Theology, and a doctorate from Harvard University. He conducts research concerning the cultural and historical background of the Bible and biblical interpretation. He is especially interested in ideas and practices that address divine-human relationships in light of suffering, loss, and trauma.

Leslie J. Hoppe, OFM, is Professor of Old Testament Studies at Catholic Theological Union in Chicago. His latest book is *Isaiah* in the New Collegeville Bible Commentary Series. He is the General Editor of the *Catholic Biblical Quarterly* and associate editor of *The Bible Today*.

Dale Launderville, OSB, is Professor of Theology at St. John's University in Collegeville, Minnesota. He has written a number of books that compare the religion of ancient Israel with that of the ancient Near East as well as ancient Greece. His latest book is *Celibacy in the Ancient World: Its Ideal and Practice in Pre-Hellenistic Israel, Mesopotamia, and Greece* (Collegeville: The Liturgical Press, 2010).

Thomas P. McCreesh, OP, has taught Old Testament at Providence College in Providence, Rhode Island, since 2005. Previously he taught for twenty-four years at the Dominican House of Studies, in Washington, DC, where he also served as president for eight years. He earned an STL (Theology) from the Dominican Houses of Studies and a PhD in Semitic Languages from The Catholic University of America, Washington, DC. He has also served as general editor of *Old Testament Abstracts*, published by the Catholic Biblical Association of America. His scholarly research has concentrated on biblical Hebrew poetry, particularly in the Wisdom tradition, as well as the prophetic literature and the psalms,

John L. McLaughlin is Associate Professor of Old Testament/Hebrew Bible at the Faculty of Theology, University of St. Michael's College and Associate Member of the Graduate Faculty, Department of Near and Middle Eastern Studies, University of Toronto. He is the author of five books, the most recent being *The Ancient Near East: An Essential Guide* (Nashville: Abingdon Press, 2012). He is currently working on *What Are They Saying About Ancient Israelite Religion?* for Paulist Press.

Irene Nowell, OSB, is a Benedictine of Mount St. Scholastica in Atchison, Kansas. She holds a master's degree in theology from St. John's University, and a doctorate in biblical studies from Catholic University and is an adjunct professor of St. John's University School of Theology. She is a past president of the Catholic Biblical Association. She has written several books and is an editor for *Give Us This Day*.

Kathleen M. O'Connor is William Marcellus McPheeters Professor of Old Testament, emerita, at Columbia Theological Seminary, Decatur, Georgia. Previously, she taught at the Maryknoll School of Theology, Ossining, New York, and has taught frequently in local churches and given courses in Central America, Thailand, Japan, and Ireland. She is author of *Jeremiah: Pain and Promise* (Fortress, 2011), *Lamentations and the Tears of the World* (Orbis, 2002), *The Wisdom Literature* (Liturgical Press, 1988), and *Job* in the New Collegeville Bible Commentary series (Liturgical Press, forthcoming). She is working on a commentary on Genesis. She is a past president of the Catholic Biblical Association of America.

Gregory J. Polan, OSB, is a Benedictine monk and priest, and the Abbot of Conception Abbey and Chancellor of Conception Seminary College where he teaches courses in Scripture and biblical languages. He served as the editor of *The Revised Grail Psalms*, and is an associate editor of *The Bible Today*.

Roberta L. Salvador, MM, has taught at St. Joseph Seminary at Dunwoodie, New York, General Theological Seminary in New York City, and Fordham University. She received her doctorate in Hebrew Bible and Ancient Semitic Languages from The Jewish Theological Seminary in New York City.

Mark S. Smith has held the Skirball Chair of Bible and Ancient Near Eastern Studies at New York University since 2000. Professor Smith completed his PhD at Yale in 1985, after taking master's degrees from the Catholic University of America, Harvard Divinity School, and Yale University. Prior to 2000, he taught at Yale University and Saint Joseph's University. He was honored as President of the Catholic Biblical Association of America in 2010–11, and in 2011 he was elected a fellow of the American Academy for Jewish Research. He has authored thirteen books and coauthored four others. His newest book is *Poetic Heroes: The Literary Commemoration of Warriors and Warrior Culture in the Early Biblical World*, to be published by Eerdmans in 2013.

Gale A. Yee is currently Nancy W. King Professor of Biblical Studies at Episcopal Divinity School, Cambridge, Massachusetts. She is the author of *Poor Banished Children of Eve: Woman as Evil in the Hebrew Bible*; *Jewish Feasts and the Gospel of John*; "The Book of Hosea" commentary in *The New Interpreter's Bible*, Vol. 7; as well as many articles and essays. She is the editor of *Judges and Method: New Approaches in Biblical Studies*, which is now in its second edition; a coeditor for the Texts@Context series and the Fortress Bible Commentary for Fortress Press (forthcoming); and former general editor of Semeia Studies.

In Memoriam

Lawrence Boadt (1942–2010) was born and raised in Los Angeles, California, and finished his college education with the Paulist Fathers in Washington, DC, at their major seminary. He was ordained a priest in 1969. His degrees include a Master of Arts in Religious Studies from St. Paul's College, Washington, DC; a Licentiate in Sacred Theology and Master of Arts in Semitic Languages from the Catholic University of America (1970, 1972); and a Licentiate and Doctorate in Sacred Scripture from the Pontifical Biblical Institute in Rome, Italy (1974, 1976). He taught in the Theology Department at Fordham University (1974–76), and at St. John's University (1975), and in the Biblical Studies Department at the Washington Theological Union, a Roman Catholic graduate school of theology in Washington, DC, from 1976 to 1997. Since 1997, he was Professor Emeritus of Biblical Studies. He served as publisher and president of Paulist Press from 1998 until his illness in 2010.

Preface

REV. LAWRENCE BOADT, CSP, FRIEND AND COLLEAGUE

Abbot Gregory J. Polan, OSB

In the summer of 1985, at the annual meeting of the Catholic Biblical Association, Christian Brother Aloysius Fitzgerald proposed to Frs. Lawrence Boadt, CSP, and Thomas McCreesh, OP, the idea of establishing an Old Testament Biblical Colloquium. The nature and purpose of this particular colloquium would be to bring together young biblical scholars who had recently completed doctoral programs and were beginning professional work in the area of Old Testament studies. It would have a threefold function: (1) to facilitate ongoing study of the Old Testament; (2) to offer mutual support and critical reviews of one another's work in the preparation of articles for publication; and (3) to periodically bring together young scholars from various areas of Old Testament studies in order to keep one another current in the ever-expanding field of research related to the ancient Near East.

At each meeting of the Colloquium, papers were to be presented by three members of the Colloquium, and a fourth paper by a senior scholar in the field. With a membership of ten to twelve persons, each member would thus be expected to present a paper every third or fourth year. Expenses would be shared equally among the members, and an annual business meeting would be conducted to determine who was to present papers and who might be invited as a visiting scholar. After a first set of invitations were issued for membership, the Old Testament Colloquium had its first meeting in late January, 1986. It continues to function to this day. It is with sadness that we acknowledge the unexpected early passing to eternity of two of its founding members: Fr. Anthony Ceresko, OSFS, (1942–2005) and Fr. Lawrence Boadt, CSP, (1942–2010).

When Larry (as he was most well-known) Boadt died, the world of biblical scholarship lost an active, energetic, and uniquely illustrious member.

His work was distinguished by superior scholarship and learning, coupled with a warmth of personality and a *joie de vivre* that infused his study of the Bible with enthusiasm and inspiration. His convictions about helping others to understand the Scriptures more fully were evident in the manner in which he presented new and challenging ideas both on the university campus and in adult education in the parish. He was forever "on fire" with the manifold topics on which he spoke. It was immediately apparent that Larry wanted his audience to understand what he had to say; at the same time he inspired his hearers to wrap their minds around new ideas that might never have occurred to them. He was a consummate teacher and an authentic missionary in the spirit of St. Paul, patron of the religious congregation of which he was a faithful and active member.

One of Larry's particular interests was to provide with his presentations a general and comprehensible overview of the various books of Scripture. He delighted in providing background information and helpful facts for someone just beginning to read a particular book of the Bible. This manifested his profound pastoral sensitivity that recognized the importance of making the Bible accessible to everyone with as much clarity as possible. Discerning textual, theological, and spiritual connections between a book's beginning and its conclusion was something that particularly intrigued Larry; he presented such insights with creativity and vigor. His foundational text for biblical studies, *Reading the Old Testament*, published in 1984 by Paulist Press, continues to be a valuable resource in classrooms both here in the United States and abroad. (This distinguished volume has only now had a "slight touch-up" by distinguished professors Rev. Richard Clifford, SJ, and Rev. Daniel Harrington, SJ.) One of Larry's special gifts was that he could render the fruit of intense scholarship in a form that was accessible, interesting, and exciting for others. A textbook by Larry Boadt garnered few if any negative comments from students who used it; it became one of those books they would keep on their shelves and return to for years to come.

Though Larry found a congenial home among the company of biblical scholars, his outreach extended far beyond his area of professional expertise. As president of Paulist Press from 1998–2009, he made exceptional use of the broad pastoral perspective from which he viewed all of life, a view that incorporated and drew from his varied interests in theology, spirituality, education, Church history, ecumenical affairs, interfaith concerns—indeed, any subject related to the Church. Meeting new people was never difficult for this affable soul; he could draw people into substantial conversations on significant topics with both humor and wisdom. From your initial meeting with Larry, you knew the things that mattered most to him: the Triune God and the Scriptures were the foundation of his work, his convictions, and his faith. And whether on matters of personal prayer, parish life, or world politics, Larry spoke with conviction, passion, and kindness.

In quiet and unobtrusive ways, Larry Boadt was a man committed to prayer. On his many visits at Conception Abbey, he might often be seen in early morning hours sitting quietly in a dimly lit corner of the abbey church as he waited for the monks to begin their morning celebrations of the Liturgy of the Hours. Though his personality was gregarious and outgoing, Larry had a quiet side that found refreshment and inner strength in quietly praying the psalms and listening to God's Word. These moments provided the fuel that powered the mighty engine of his scholarly and apostolic endeavors.

In what concerns Larry Boadt's publications, his legacy was outstanding. He was the author of several books, including *Ezekiel's Oracles against Egypt* (Biblical Institute Press, 1980); a study of the poetic techniques of ancient Near Eastern prophecy; two commentaries in the Old Testament Message series, published by Michael Glazier, Inc.: *Jeremiah 1–25* (1982), and *Jeremiah 26–52, Habakkuk, Zephaniah and Nahum* (1983); a general introduction to the Hebrew Scriptures titled *Reading the Old Testament: An Introduction* (Paulist Press, 1985); and *Introduction to Wisdom Literature, Proverbs,* Collegeville Bible Commentary 18 (Liturgical Press, 1986).

Other major scholarly publications include the entries "Ezekiel" for the *New Jerome Biblical Commentary* (Prentice-Hall, 1990); "Ezekiel" in the *Anchor Bible Dictionary* (1992); "Introduction to the Pentateuch" in the *Oxford Catholic Study Bible of the New American Bible* (1992; 2003); and articles on Hebrew poetry and prophetic texts in various books and such leading scholarly journals as the *Catholic Biblical Quarterly,* the *Journal of Biblical Literature,* and *Vetus Testamentum.*

Popular publications include two audiocassette series on the introduction to the Bible, "Towards Understanding the Old Testament," and "Towards Understanding the New Testament"; articles on biblical topics for *The Bible Today;* lectionary aids for preaching in numerous series; general editorship of the Paulist Bible Study Program; a series of sixty-four videocassettes on biblical topics; "The Introduction to the Bible" for the Raleigh, North Carolina, diocesan television series; an "Introduction to the Old Testament" for CTNA (Catholic Television Network of America) and others; biblical commentaries for *Religion in the News* radio programs; and numerous biblical articles for *The Catholic World* magazine. Beginning in 1997, he produced eight audiocassette introductions to various books of the Old Testament for Alba House Publications. In 2002, he was editor of the volume *Why I Am a Priest,* and his *The Life of Saint Paul* was released in 2008. Larry even wrote a children's picture book, simple yet insightful Christmas meditations called *Stations of the Nativity,* illustrated by Patrick Kelley (2002). These last three titles were all published by Paulist Press.

The articles in this present volume are written by his fellow members of the Old Testament Colloquium. Each essay is designed to be used in lay settings (parish book clubs, Bible studies, undergraduate courses). Each essay directs readers to particular biblical texts that will be discussed in the essay. The essays address the Bible in the modern world, and end with questions for personal reflection or group discussion. Bibliographies are also provided for further reading.

Larry Boadt's passing was a great loss for colleagues, friends, and fellow religious, a bereavement deeply felt by all who knew and loved him. This volume honors not only Larry Boadt, but also that great work that was so important to him: bringing the Bible to life for each and every person who sought in the sacred texts a word of strength and hope. May Larry's vibrant spirit and authentic love for the Word of God live on in all who were touched by his words and example.

Chapter 1

WHY DO WE HAVE SO MANY TRANSLATIONS OF THE BIBLE?

Irene Nowell, OSB

TAKE A MOMENT TO COMPARE THESE TRANSLATIONS OF GENESIS 1:1–3:

When God began to create heaven and earth—the earth being unformed and void, with darkness over the surface of the deep and a wind from God sweeping over the water—God said, "Let there be light"; and there was light. (*Jewish Publication Society*)

In the beginning, when God created the heavens and the earth—and the earth was without form or shape, with darkness over the abyss and a mighty wind sweeping over the waters—Then God said: Let there be light, and there was light. (*New American Bible Revised Edition*)

In the beginning when God created the heavens and the earth, the earth was a formless void and darkness covered the face of the deep, while a wind from God swept over the face of the waters. Then God said, "Let there be light"; and there was light. (*New Revised Standard Version*)

I am often asked why we have so many translations. Shouldn't the Bible always stay the same? The answer is yes and no. In order to ensure that the truth of the biblical message remains clear for each generation, translations need continually to be revised to keep up with the language of the people. Such translation projects have occupied most of my professional life. For many years I had the privilege of working with Fr. Lawrence Boadt on the International Commission for English in the Liturgy (ICEL) Psalter Project. At the same time, I was working on a revision of the psalms for the New American Bible, and Larry teased me about working at cross-purposes. But I learned much from him and am grateful for the experience.

Why are scholars and theologians still taking on the task of translating the Bible? Why do we have so many translations, with new ones still appearing every so often? In a paper written in the 1980s, Fr. Boadt outlines the reasons:

> Language changes, word usage shifts dramatically, and the need for new translations constantly arises. Moreover, in this [twentieth] century, scholarship has discovered so many new texts from ancient Semitic peoples that our lexicographic stock and knowledge of Semitic grammar has ballooned, revealing the extreme inadequacy of many words and passages in the Douay-Rheims translation, for example. (Paper on Approach to Translation, 3)

Boadt also points out the diversity of audiences and the variety of styles of translation. These same issues still drive the need for new translations and will continue to do so into the future.

THE TEXT

Where do we begin? For the Old Testament, the answer seems deceptively obvious: the Hebrew "original," of course. The problem, is that we do not have the "original" for any of the biblical books. The best Hebrew manuscripts date from the late tenth to early eleventh centuries AD. But there are other sources. Old Testament books were translated into Greek beginning around the mid-third century BC. The manuscripts we have of that Greek translation, called the Septuagint, move us several centuries closer to the original. But more complexities arise. Not one but several Greek translations began to circulate. (Sound familiar?)

The Greek translators, helpful as they were, still had their difficulties. First of all, they had the same difficulty we experience. Which text to translate? At the time of their work there were various Hebrew versions of biblical books such as Psalms and Jeremiah. The Hebrew text was not yet standardized. Also, the Greek language has a much larger vocabulary than biblical Hebrew. Several Greek words were necessary to pick up the connotations of one Hebrew word. These translators also made some mistakes. Hebrew is written basically with consonants only. So the Hebrew root *dbr* can be spelled *dabar*, which means "word" or "thing," and it can also be spelled *deber*, which means "plague" or "pestilence." So in Hosea, the phrase "Death, where are your plagues?" becomes "Death, where is your judgment [i.e., word]?" (Hos 13:14). In Habakkuk we find, "Before his face went a *word*" instead of "Before him went pestilence" (Hab 3:5). Psalm 90/91:3 reads: "He will deliver me from the snare of the hunter and from the *word* of the one who terrifies." The Hebrew means, "and from the deadly pestilence."

Also these Greek translators adapted the text to fit the culture of their audience. Instead of translating literally the list of finery in Isaiah 3:18–23, the Greek translator listed the finery worn by women in his place and time. Instead of "signet rings and nose rings" we find garments with "purple edges and purple weave." "Turbans and shawls" become garments "interwoven with blue [hyacinth] and flowing summer clothes." Origen, a third-century Christian scholar, attempted to systematize these Greek translations around AD 230 by putting them in parallel columns next to a Hebrew text.

By the mid-second century the Bible began to be translated into Latin, usually from the Greek Septuagint. Many Latin versions began to circulate, which led Pope Damasus (366–384) to ask St. Jerome to make a definitive Latin version. Jerome began with two early versions of the Book of Psalms, a simple revision and a translation from the Greek. Then he began the major work of translating the whole Bible, Old Testament and New Testament. He decided to translate the Old Testament from available *Hebrew* texts (and some Aramaic). This decision led to a serious disagreement between St. Jerome and St. Augustine, who insisted that the *Greek* Septuagint was the standard Christian Bible. But Jerome persevered in his decision. His work, called the Vulgate ("for the common people"), was designated as the approved version, but the various Old Latin translations also remained in circulation until the eighth–ninth century.

So through most of the early Middle Ages Christians had several translations of the Bible available to them. Their situation was not unlike our own. A new challenge presented itself in the sixteenth century with the Reformation and the Counter Reformation. The reformers began the long tradition of translating Scripture into the language of the people, while the Catholic Church decreed that the Latin Vulgate was the standard text, although some translations were made. This will be discussed in further detail in the section on families of translations.

NEW DISCOVERIES

Two new discoveries in the modern era radically shifted the situation. First of all, in the nineteenth century several fragments of Hebrew manuscripts were found in a synagogue in Cairo, Egypt. They were in a *geniza*, a hiding place where worn scrolls were placed so they would not be desecrated. These scrolls dated to the sixth–eighth centuries AD and thus gave access to much older witnesses to the Hebrew text. Some of these fragments were from the Book of Sirach, or Ecclesiasticus. This long Wisdom book, written around 175 BC by a Jewish sage, had not been included in the Jewish canon of Scripture when their list of sacred books was finally closed. So the Hebrew text was no longer copied and was eventually lost. Christians, however, were using the book in its Greek translation, which had been made by the grandson of the writer several decades later. (The book went through other translations into Syriac and Latin, and each group of translators changed and added to the text.) Now, since portions of the Hebrew text have become available, a comparison can be made between the grandfather's work and the grandson's translation. This comparison reveals a shift in theological belief. Ben Sira, the writer, did not have a belief in life after death, but his grandson did. So the grandson edited his grandfather's work. For example, Sirach 7:17 reads in Hebrew:

> More and more, humble your pride;
> What awaits mortals is worms. (NABRE)

But in Greek it reads:

> Humble yourself to the utmost,
> For the punishment of the ungodly is fire and worms. (NRSV)

In the Hebrew version everyone, all mortals, can expect only worms and the grave at death. Ben Sira believed that everyone, good and bad, went to a place called Sheol. But in the Greek translation it is only the ungodly who will experience this destruction, and now fire is added to their fate. The grandson believes in life after death and also heaven and hell. Because of this shift in belief, his version differs from his grandfather's. So the twenty-first-century translators must now decide which of these two versions to translate.

Another major discovery in recent times happened near the Dead Sea at a place called Qumran. Beginning in 1947, many scrolls and fragments of scrolls were discovered in a series of caves. These scrolls date from the third century BC to the mid-first century AD. They are thus a millennium older than the best Hebrew texts translators have been using. So, did this simplify the translators' task? No! In fact, it complicated it. What the scholars studying the scrolls discovered was not a definitive text, but a multiplicity of versions of various biblical books. The text had not yet been standardized. The gift of the scrolls was a glimpse into the history of the transmission of the text. For example, the large psalms scroll found in Cave 11 has most of the psalms in the order that we know up to Psalm 90. But from that point on there are other prayer-poems as well as familiar psalms, but not in the order that we expect. Apparently the final third of the Book of Psalms was not yet fixed.

The Qumran scrolls also helped translators with puzzling texts, however. One such text is Psalm 122:3. The standard Hebrew text reads:

Jerusalem, built as a city that is joined to her [Hebrew *lah*].

So what does "joined to her" mean? The nearest feminine antecedent is Jerusalem. So most translations say something like "bound firmly together" (NRSV) or "walled round about" (NABRE) or "bonded as one together" (Revised Grail). But Lawrence Boadt pointed out that a Qumran scroll (11QPsa) had "joined to *him* [*lo*]," not "joined to *her*." He proposed that the antecedent for "him" was the temple, the "house of the LORD" in verse 1. So the ICEL translation reads:

Jerusalem, the city so built that city and temple are one.

A happy solution!

THE PRESENT SITUATION: CHALLENGES

So why are scholars and theologians still taking on the task of translating the Bible? Why do we have so many translations, with new ones still appearing every so often? Boadt pointed out that we need new translations because of language changes, shifts in word usage, different audiences, styles of translation, and new insights from these recent discoveries.

A living language changes. Every year new words are added to the lexicon. Many of them will not find their way into biblical translations, but some will. Other words take on new meanings. The word "suffer," used in earlier biblical translations to mean "allow," no longer has that connotation. So the phrase "Suffer little children, and forbid them not, to come unto me" (Matt 19:14 KJV) can be misinterpreted to mean that children must experience pain, an interpretation used with terrible consequences in *Sophie's Choice*. The word "holocaust" has also taken on a horrific meaning in our time, so newer translations use the phrase "burnt offering." Some words are no longer in current English, such as "thee" and "thou," "doth" and "hath." Paradoxically the pronouns that once were informal, "thee" and "thou," have now became formal and were eventually dropped from the language. Sometimes it is simply the case that the idiom has changed. My students laughed me out of the room for talking about "booty," which now has a slang connotation I did not intend. Finally, no matter how hard the translators work, every translation has awkward or misleading expressions. The story of Jacob's flight from his father-in-law Laban was reported this way in the NAB:

> Jacob proceeded to put his children and wives on camels, and he drove off with all his livestock and all the property he had acquired in Paddan-aram, to go to his father Isaac in the land of Canaan. (Gen 31:17–18)

The image that immediately comes to mind (at least for a Midwesterner) is that of the family going off on camels and Jacob driving the truck loaded with livestock. In the new version it is revised to read:

> Jacob proceeded to put his children and wives on camels, and he drove off all his livestock and all the property he had acquired in Paddan-aram, to go to his father Isaac in the land of Canaan. (NABRE)

If Scripture is to be a living Word speaking to this generation, the vocabulary and modes of expression must keep pace.

Sometimes the text is ambiguous, and every group of translators must make a decision concerning the meaning. Psalm 104 describes God's great work of creation in terms of the mythological defeat of the waters. Verses 5 to 7 say:

> You set the earth on its foundation,
> immovable from age to age.
> You wrapped it with the depths like a cloak;
> the waters stood higher than the mountains.
> At your threat they took to flight;
> at the voice of your thunder they fled. (Revised Grail)

The next verse has only four words in the first line; the translations are indicated here with hyphens and slashes between each word for clarity. In order they read:

> they-rose-up / the-mountains / they-went-down / the-valleys

So the real question is: What went up? Is it the waters in their rush to get away from God's rebuke? Is it the mountains as the waters receded? And what went down? The waters again? Or the valleys as the mountains rose? The text can be read in any of those ways. In one of the translation groups in which I participated, one excellent seasoned scholar argued passionately for one reading and another equally excellent seasoned scholar argued vehemently for the other. One insisted that nothing in the psalms was against the laws of nature, so the mountains went up and the waters went down. The other argued that this was mythological reality and the fleeing waters went up the mountains and down into the valleys. The argument went on for two days. In the end, the mythological view won out. Psalm 104:8 in NABRE reads:

> They [the waters] rushed up the mountains, down the valleys
> to the place you had fixed for them.

But the other viewpoint is represented in the Revised Grail Psalms:

> The mountains rose, the valleys descended,
> to the place which you had appointed them.

We are fortunate to have both to remind us that much of the biblical text is still ambiguous.

Besides language changes and ambiguities, translators are faced with the variety of experiences and cultural realities of the target audience. This challenge faced even the earliest translators, as we saw above when the scribe who translated Isaiah 3 into Greek substituted his own list of fineries for the Hebrew list. He obviously wanted his own audience to relate to the prophet's criticism.

Theological beliefs change, as we saw in the comparison of Ben Sira and his grandson. In the years between them a faith in life after death had developed and the grandson, true to his belief and that of his audience, changed his grandfather's text (Sir 7:17). St. Jerome read the Old Testament prophets from a Christian viewpoint. So, for example, he translated Haggai 2:7 thus:

> And I will move all nations: AND THE DESIRED OF ALL
> NATIONS SHALL COME: and I will fill this house with glory:
> saith the Lord of hosts. (Douay-Rheims)

We recognize the phrase "desired of nations" from the Advent hymn, "O Come, O Come, Emmanuel." Jerome has interpreted the Hebrew to refer to a coming messiah. The original meaning, which would have made sense to the prophet's audience, is usually interpreted to be the "treasures of the nations," which will be brought to the new temple:

> I will shake all the nations,
> so that the treasures of all the nations will come in.
> And I will fill this house with glory—
> says the LORD of hosts. (NABRE)

METHODS OF TRANSLATION:
PURPOSE AND AUDIENCE

Every biblical translation is intended to achieve certain ends. Boadt lists these as (1) an accurate rendering of the original text; (2) a translation that conveys the spirit of the original text; (3) a reading that makes sense in the modern language, the target language of the translation; (4) a reading that has literary quality; and, perhaps the most difficult challenge, (5) a translation that will produce the same effect in the modern reader that the original produced in its audience (3). But there are different ways to achieve these ends. Thus translators use different methods, depending on the purpose of the translation and the audience for which it is intended.

A major factor in the method of translation is the purpose for which a particular biblical translation is intended. In his essay Boadt calls this the "finality" of the project (3). Translations intended for study are usually prepared according to formal correspondence. The scholar or student seeks a translation that will reveal the bones of the original language. The translator attempts to be faithful to grammatical or poetic units and to be consistent in the translation of specific words or phrases. A mechanical one-for-one translation of these words, however, is neither possible nor desirable. Often the target language has a larger vocabulary than the original language. Nuances and idioms are not identical. Theological insights develop. Examples of ancient translations that take these differences into account are the Greek translations of Isaiah 3:18–23 and Sirach 7:17 described above. Literary techniques are often impossible to replicate in the target language. Puns do not work in another language. The Hebrew poetic techniques of alliteration (repeating the same beginning letter in several consecutive words) or acrostic (beginning each line with the next letter of the alphabet) are virtually impossible to achieve without altering the meaning of the text.

A second method of translation is dynamic equivalence. The focus in this method is the response of the reader or hearer. An attempt is made to render the text as accurately as possible in language that recipients will immediately understand and will recognize as their own normal speech patterns. Translators using this method also strive to be faithful to the meaning of the text and to the literary forms of poetry and prose. But, when a term or phrase is proposed, they also frequently ask: "When was the last time you heard that word in ordinary conversation or read it in the newspaper?" This method is used in translations intended for audiences such as children or those for whom English is a second language, but it is also used effectively in translations intended for prayer or meditative reading.

A third factor, which influences translations using either of the above methods, has to do with translations intended for public worship, whether sung or read. This factor applies most often to translations of the psalms.

Attention must be paid to the length of lines, to the rhythm of the words, to consonant combinations that are difficult to sing, and to complex grammatical constructions.

TRADITION/FAMILIES OF TRANSLATIONS

Several families of translation have developed in response to these needs and these methods of translation. The following are based on the method of formal equivalence.

Although there were earlier translations of the Christian Bible into English, the King James Bible holds pride of place as the most long lasting. In their fidelity to Hebrew idiom, these translators reinvented the English language. Translations following in the King James tradition are the Revised Standard Version (RSV, 1952), and the New Revised Standard Version (NRSV, 1989). These translations also remain very close to the Hebrew text, with some emendations from the Greek. The language is elegant.

Some examples from the beginning of Psalm 8 will illustrate the characteristics and progression of these translations. Note the move from "thy/thou" to "you/your" and from "sucklings" to "infants," a more common term for babies. For the second line, the NRSV translators returned to the KJV version, considering it more accurate. By using "Sovereign" in the first line, they also make it clear that these first two words of the psalm are different Hebrew words. One is the sacred name of God; the other is the ordinary term for "lord" or "master."

> O LORD our Lord, how excellent is thy name in all the earth!
> who hast set thy glory above the heavens.
> Out of the mouth of babes and sucklings
> hast thou ordained strength because of thy enemies,
> that thou mightest still the enemy and the avenger. (KJV)

> O LORD, our Lord, how majestic is thy name in all the earth!
> Thou whose glory above the heavens is chanted
> by the mouth of babes and infants,
> thou has founded a bulwark because of thy foes,
> to still the enemy and the avenger. (RSV)

> O LORD, our Sovereign, how majestic is your name in all the earth!
> You have set your glory above the heavens.
> Out of the mouths of babes and infants
> you have founded a bulwark because of your foes,
> to silence the enemy and the avenger. (NRSV)

The Catholic tradition has a different history. In 1546 the Council of Trent mandated the Latin Vulgate as the standard text. Older Catholics will remember the readings at Mass being proclaimed in Latin. English-speaking Catholics needed an English Bible, however, and the Douay-Rheims translation of the Vulgate filled that need. Only in the mid-twentieth century did Pope Pius XII authorize Catholic scholars to translate Scripture from the Hebrew and Greek versions. The firstfruits of that effort appeared under the auspices of the Confraternity of Christian Doctrine, the Confraternity Version (1941). That version grew into the New American Bible (NAB, 1970) and its newly revised version (NABRE, 2011). This tradition too remains close to the Hebrew and Greek texts, but also makes a serious attempt to use the idiom of American English. Another translation in the Catholic tradition is the Jerusalem Bible (1966, 1973) and its revised version, the New Jerusalem Bible (NJB, 1985). This began as a French translation and, even though the NJB is translated from the original languages, it retains its French elegance and Latinate roots.

The Jewish Publication Society published a new translation of the Hebrew Bible in 1985, *Tanakh*. This translation remains very close to the received text in Hebrew. Unlike most translations made under Christian auspices, *Tanakh* makes virtually no emendations from the ancient Greek translations.

Examples of Psalm 51:4–5 in these translations show development and the variety of ways the text may be translated. "Iniquity" in the Douay-Rheims translation becomes the more familiar word "guilt" in the New American Bible tradition and the Jerusalem Bible, but the Jewish Publication Society prefers "iniquity." NAB and NABRE follow the Douay-Rheims with "cleanse," from a Germanic root, whereas the Jerusalem Bible and the NJB prefer "purify," from a Latin root.

> Wash me yet more from my iniquity, and cleanse me from my sin,
> For I know my iniquity, and my sin is always before me.
>   (Douay-Rheims)

> Thoroughly wash me from my guilt
> and of my sin cleanse me.
> For I acknowledge my offense,
> and my sin is before me always. (NAB)

> Thoroughly wash away my guilt;
> and from my sin cleanse me.
> For I know my transgressions;
> my sin is always before me. (NABRE)

Wash me clean of my guilt,
purify me from my sin.
For I am well aware of my faults,
I have my sin constantly in mind. (JB)

Wash me thoroughly from my guilt,
purify me from my sin.
For I am well aware of my offences,
my sin is constantly in mind. (NJB)

Wash me thoroughly of my iniquity,
and purify me of my sin;
for I recognize my transgressions,
and am ever conscious of my sin. (JPS)

Translations using the method of dynamic equivalence continue to appear. The Good News Translation (GNT) began in 1966 with a translation of the New Testament: *Good News for Modern Man*. It is designed to be easily read by people for whom English is a second language. The vocabulary was limited to certain words and grammatical constructions were held to simpler structures. A translation of the New Testament, called originally *God's Word to the Nations*, appeared in 1998. (It was eventually renamed the *New Evangelical Translation*.) A completely new translation of the whole Bible, called *God's Word*, was published in 1995. The intent is "a translation of the Scriptures presented in the clear, natural English of today," in other words, a translation based on the method of dynamic equivalence.

The Living Bible (1971) moves one step further away from formal correspondence and toward idiomatic English. It is an attempt to make Scripture clear to children and is a paraphrase of English versions. There is also a Catholic edition, *The Way*, which adds the books that do not appear in Protestant Bibles, such as Judith and Tobit.

Examples of Psalm 51:2–3 in these translations show various ways to bring the biblical Word into contemporary language. The most interesting examples are in the final phrase: "I am always conscious of my sins" (GNT); "my sin is always in front of me" (*God's Word*); "they haunt me day and night" (New Living Translation).

Wash away all my evil
and make me clean from my sin!
I recognize my faults;
I am always conscious of my sins. (GNT)

Wash me thoroughly from my guilt,
and cleanse me from my sin.
I admit that I am rebellious.
My sin is always in front of me. (God's Word)

Wash me clean from my guilt.
Purify me from my sin,
For I recognize my shameful deeds—
they haunt me day and night. (NLT)

Two translations of the psalms deserve mention, one following the method of formal correspondence and the other the method of dynamic equivalence. First of all, in 1963 the Grail, a women's community in England, published a translation of the psalms designed to be sung. An attempt was made to imitate the rhythm of the Hebrew text and the psalms were set to the psalm tones of Joseph Gelineau. This translation became the one that most Catholics knew through the end of the twentieth century. Several minor revisions were made through the years, but in 2008 a complete revision was made in the light of new standards set by the Vatican document *Liturgiam authenticam*. The translation, the *Revised Grail Psalter*, follows the Hebrew text more closely but remains beautifully poetic and quite singable. Abbot Gregory Polan, OSB, made the revision. This translation has been approved for Catholic liturgical worship.

The other translation of the Book of Psalms was sponsored by ICEL. A sizeable committee was assembled to translate the psalms into idiomatic English (the dynamic equivalence method), which was also suited for singing. Fr. Lawrence Boadt was on that committee, as was I. The method allowed us to present the psalms with shorter lines, as the Hebrew text does, and to offer a translation different from the other options in circulation.

Examples of Psalm 51 in these translations:

Wash me completely from my iniquity,
and cleanse me from my sin.
My transgressions, truly I know them;
my sin is always before me. (Revised Grail)

Wash away my sin,
cleanse me from my guilt.
I know my evil well,
it stares me in the face. (ICEL)

CONCLUSION

So why are there so many translations of the Bible, with new ones coming out frequently? First, the texts to be translated are varied, and new discoveries have been made and possibly still will be. Second, English is a living language and thus continues to develop and change. New words, new meanings, new idioms continue to appear. Third, theological insights are still being honed and the wonders of God's revelation are new every day. Fourth, worship traditions and practices continue to call for new and better translations. It seems unlikely that translators will run out of work any time soon.

QUESTIONS

1. What translation of the Bible do you use for reading and prayer? Do you use more than one translation?

2. Do you have a favorite translation of Psalm 23 or another beloved passage? Why do you like that particular translation?

3. If you read another translation do you get new insights into the meaning of the biblical passage?

BIBLIOGRAPHY

Boadt, Lawrence. "Paper on Approach to Translation." Documentation for ICEL Translation Project. Unpublished.

Daniell, David. *The Bible in English: Its History and Influence*. New Haven, CT: Yale University Press, 2003.

Kugel, James L. *The Bible As It Was*. Cambridge, MA: Belknap Press of Harvard University Press, 1997.

McGrath, Alister. *In the Beginning: The Story of the King James Bible and How It Changed a Nation, a Language, and a Culture*. New York: Doubleday, 2001.

Nicolson, Adam. *God's Secretaries: The Making of the King James Bible*. New York: HarperCollins, 2003.

Nowell, Irene. "The Making of Translations: A Dilemma." *Worship* 75 (2001): 58–68.

Würthwein, Ernst. *The Text of the Old Testament*. Translated by Erroll F. Rhodes. Grand Rapids, MI: Eerdmans, 1979.

Chapter 2

WHY READ THE STORY IN THE GARDEN?

Kathleen M. O'Connor

READ GENESIS 2–3

People live by stories. Without them we do not know who we are individually or communally; we lose our bearings in the world; we have no past nor can we find a clear path toward the future. The Book of Genesis provides stories that lie at the root of our identities as believing communities. Among these, the story of the Garden of Eden (2:4—3:24) holds an iconic place in our culture, even among nonbelievers. But what does it really say? Popular thinking often reduces this two-part story to a literal report about the creation of the first couple, or a simple tale about the origins of original sin, or sometimes uses it as an excuse to blame women for the evils of the world. Although the Garden story stands as a companion to the account of creation in seven days (Gen 1:1—2:3), this one haunts Western imagination and can seem as simple as a children's tale, but what happens when we read it with close attention?

To read Genesis 2–3 carefully is to find new questions such as: Who are we, and how are we related to God and to other parts of creation? Why is there attraction between the sexes? Why is life so painful? Why do we die? Does God intend that men should rule over women?

The story of the Garden is not a children's story but a richly tapestried narrative with many levels of meaning. Its drama, characters, memorable plot, and deceptive simplicity can draw us into a playful yet profound view of life with God in the world. To read it carefully is to uncover layers of beauty, as well as unfathomable questions, and the way the story unfolds reflects that complexity. It is creative and playful, filled with conflicts, and consequences,

15

with wordplay and irony, and with conversations that reverberate in adult lives at many levels today.

Life in the Garden takes place as a drama in two acts. Act 1: "It's a Beautiful World" (2:4b–25) sets up a network of peaceful relationships, an integrated web of life, a vision of congenial agreements among creatures. Act 2: "It's a Broken World" (3:1–24) tells of a cascading set of disruptions that force questions upon us about the nature of human life and our relationship to the Creator. Each act of the drama divides into smaller scenes.

ACT 1: "IT'S A BEAUTIFUL WORLD" (GENESIS 2:4b–25)

The first scene opens at a vague time and place, the time "when God created the heavens and the earth." What marks this time and place is its near emptiness, when neither shrub nor grass had sprung up, when there was neither rain nor human to till the ground. The narrator—the omniscient voice telling the story—emphasizes what is missing: life is missing from the dry, uninhabited landscape. But then a stream would "rise up and water the whole face of the ground" (2:6). Into blank emptiness comes the prerequisite for any life in the form of rain and a stream of water.

The first creative act of God in this story is to reverse barrenness, to prepare conditions for life, to transform a dusty deathscape into a fertile place. Yet the story shows God at work behind the scenes. God establishes a climate in which life might burst. God's creativity is subtle, hidden and revealed at once, generating life where there is none. The eruption of the waters into the desert solves the first problem in the story. The barren land is ready for transformation, but the story delays reporting that transformation until God makes a human from the dust of the ground (2:7).

The First Human (2:7)

The literary depth of the story becomes clear when we notice plays on words that occur across these two chapters. Evident in the Hebrew text, the wordplays are hard to translate into English, but knowing they are there reveals the story's playfulness and gives us a sense of the nature of the literature. It is an entertainment of great seriousness. The first play on words appears when God forms humankind (*adam*) from the dust of the ground (*adamah*, 2:7). The word translated "man," or more precisely "human," closely resembles the word for "ground" from which God formed him. At this point in the story, Adam is a kind of androgynous figure, not yet identified as male though by the time chapter 2 ends Adam is clearly a male. The narrator presents us with an unspecified human, though ancient readers would surely have identified the character as male. *Adamah*, the word translated "ground," looks like a feminine form of *adam*. Similar in spelling and sound, the two words play off each other to convey profound interconnection between humans and the earth. The one is made from the other; the raw material of humanity is the ground itself. Relationship between humans and the ground is primal, substantive, and awesome.

Yet humans and the earth are not equivalent in importance. God distinguishes Adam from the ground by breathing "the breath [*ruah*] of life" into his nostrils. The Hebrew word for "breath" also means "wind" or "spirit." When God breathes into Adam's nostrils, God does more than merely ignite life within the creature; God adds the spirit of divine life, God's own breath, to the human body, making Adam a participant in God's own life. Adam breathes the breath of God. This is something like the claim of the previous creation story where, on the sixth day, God makes humans in the divine image.

> God created mankind in his image;
> *in the image of God he created them;*
> *male and female he created them.* (Gen 1:26–27)

In the Garden, the human participates in the breath or spirit of God, even as he is also made from the dust of the ground. It is the breath of God that turns the human from a lump of earth into a living person. To be human, then, is to be simultaneously of the ground and of God.

The Garden (2:8–14)

Only after God creates the human does the landscape come back into focus. God plants a Garden in Eden and makes trees grow from the ground, "every tree that was delightful to look at and good for food" (2:9). And there, in that verdant Garden, God places the human. Among the trees, God plants two particular ones, "the tree of life…and the tree of the knowledge of good and evil." Even though the trees have no role in act 1, the narrator mentions them now in good storytelling fashion, and then tells of the divine prohibition against eating from them (vv. 15–17). These glimpses of the special trees create suspense, suggest that something mysterious is hidden in the Garden, and, of course, they foreshadow key events in the next chapter (3:1–24).

The next scene locates the Garden in the east and emphasizes its oasis-like quality. It is an island bounded by a four rivers, one on each side (vv. 10–14). Of the rivers, two are known—the Tigris and the Euphrates—while the other two have no clear geographical parallels, implying that the Garden is firmly on the earth yet also a mythic place. Wherever the Garden lies, though, its river-fed location makes it a place of green, ripe life, an idyllic oasis, beautiful and rich even with gold and fine stones. Fertility promised by the presence of the waters in the first scene comes to full expression here.

The narrator reports again that God settled the human in the Garden. God plants the Garden and then gives him a purpose already hinted at in verse five. He is "to cultivate the soil and care for it" (v.15). He is to become the gardener, worker, and steward. The word translated "cultivate" or "till" also means "to serve." Cultivating the soil is a form of service, a work of reverence to and stewardship of the ground. From the beginning, according to this story, God intends for humans to work. Work, "keeping" or "caring for" the earth, is a gift of God, not a form of punishment. Work constitutes the human vocation.

Adam Alone (2:18–23)

But another difficulty arises in the Garden (2:18–23). Without a problem to solve or a conflict to settle, there would be no real story, no tension nor excitement, only a listing of events. The major problem of the first act is that the human is alone. God, not the human, notices that "it is not good for man to be alone" (v. 18). But this problem is more intractable than that of barren landscape (vv. 4–6), for not just any solution will do. God sets particular conditions for solving it: "I will make a helper suited to him." In the Old Testament, to be a helper is to be like God who is the "helper" of Israel (Ps 46:2 and Deut 33:7). Adam's helper must be "suited to him," according to his kind, one like him, one who helps him as God helps humans, and perhaps who, in the best of all worlds, receives help in return. But the problem of Adam's aloneness takes more than one effort to be solved. God's first attempt (vv. 19–20) is not satisfactory, and again in good storytelling style, the delay in finding a solution builds tension and highlights the creation of the woman as the climax to act 1.

In the initial attempt to find a helper, God repeats one of the steps used to create the human in the first place. God takes the ground and from it forms the wild animals and birds and brings them to the human to appraise, "but none proved to be a helper suited to him" (v. 19). Note that God omits the divine breath as an ingredient of the animals' creation. They do not participate in divine life in the same way the human does, and that means they are not "suited to him," not according to his kind. Yet Adam is closely connected to the animals. He and the animals are made from the ground, and he gets to name them. Some interpreters think that in the ancient world the one naming gains power and control over the ones named, but I do not agree. I think Adam recognizes the distinctive essence of each animal, and so can call each by name in respectful relationship. The human connects with animals, but in this story, they are not equal to the human.

To avoid a failed second attempt to solve the problem of Adam's alone-ness, God puts the human asleep and extracts a rib directly from his body (v. 21). This time God begins with the same human substance that composes Adam's body, bone made from the ground and from divine breath. With the rib bone as a starting point—that is, with the material made from the ground and from divine breath—God forms the woman. There can be no mistake this time; she is suited to him, according to his kind, of the same ground-spirit mixture. Adam confirms her suitability and likeness to him in a burst of poetic song:

> "This at last is bone of my bone
> and flesh of my flesh." (2:23)

When a biblical narrative switches from prose to poetry, the genre change usually marks an important moment, an occasion that draws attention. When Adam speaks in astonished poetry, it is to honor and celebrate the exis-tence of the woman and to affirm God's creation as suitable to him. His excla-mation that they are of the same flesh and bone uses words that appear elsewhere in the Old Testament. When the people of Israel proclaim David to be their king in covenant with him, they say he is of their bone and flesh (2 Sam 5:1; 19:12, 13). This is language of kinship, of mutual relationship, of honor and responsibility. When Adam speaks of the woman standing before him, he dou-bles the nouns, "bone of my bone, flesh of my flesh," in a superlative exclama-tion of her suitability. Then, to highlight the closeness of their relationship, another wordplay appears. The word for "woman" (*ishah*) is nearly identical in Hebrew to the word meaning "her man" (*ish*). Adam's poetic outburst expresses his delight in his sexual partner and conveys, by the nearly identical spelling and sound, their identity and union with one another.

Adam's poetic jubilation highlights the event toward which the story has been pressing, the creation of the woman as his partner, and lest we doubt it, the narrator adds a moral to the story, a "that-is-why" statement to hammer home the meaning. That is why a man leaves his parents and "clings to his wife [woman] and the two of them become one body" (v. 24).

The first act of the story in the Garden "explains" the origins of sexual attraction between two people who are of the "same kind," that is, suitable to one another. Sex is central to the divine plan, a gift of God, a primal element of creation. That the story is about heterosexual marriage may be assumed in the ancient world, but marriage here is not the primary point, even though the NABRE translates woman as "wife" rather than "woman." It is primarily about the rootedness of sexual attraction in the creativity of God. The story is a creative celebration of the fact of sex, not yet about children or the pass-ing on of life to future generations. The story honors sexual life because the couple signifies the high point of divine creativity in act 1.

Yet the first act is not yet over. One more verse adds another larger layer of meaning to the story; both the man and the woman were naked, "yet they felt no shame" (v. 25). As a final detail, the last verse reaches back to the whole chapter as a veiled summary of the story about the beautiful world. The two figures are unashamed of their bodies. They are whole and integrated in themselves. They live in complete openness before one another like innocent children. Nothing is amiss within or without in this Garden. Comfortable with and accepting of themselves as embodied beings, they are also at peace with their surroundings, with the animals, and with God.

The first act portrays a beautiful world. It offers a glimpse of the way the world seems when one is falling in love, or when all seems well and in harmonious balance. The chapter provides a glimpse of peace, joy, and right relationship of humans within themselves, with each other, with the ground, with the animals, and with the Creator God. On our rare best days, the world may seem this way but not for long. Inevitably a different, less ideal reality sets in, and we encounter other darker experiences. Unlike the previous account where creation occurs in seven days (Gen 1:1—2:3), this story never says creation is "good" or "very good." Instead, Genesis 2 shows that creation is good and beautiful, and the work of God. It suggests that such an interrelated, harmonious world is God's intention. The Garden story turns out to be a many-splendored narrative about the kind of world God intends. In it, God is deeply involved with the processes of creation—forming, shaping, planting, sending water, solving problems, providing food, celebrating sex. The story builds to the creation of sexuality and celebrates sexual differentiation and union. And it exalts and honors humans by presenting them as part earth and part divine breath.

But the first act of this drama is also a literary setup, a starting point where all things are good and beautiful, but it does not exist; it is unreal or perhaps only momentarily true. Yet the chapter builds hope that such a world might one day exist in more than in a veiled glimpse. But when a story begins at the height of idyllic harmony, the only place it can go is downward.

ACT 2: "IT'S A BROKEN WORLD" (GENESIS 3:1–24)

The second act also unfolds in smaller scenes, the first of which introduces a new character, the snake (3:1–7). As the plot develops in this half of the story, every harmonious element set up in the first act disintegrates.

The Snake (3:1–7)

The fact of a talking snake with which chapter 3 begins gives us another clue to the story's nature. It is not realistic in style but mythic, a story to provoke amazement and invite questions. The snake appears out of the blue, one of the wild animals in God's green Garden. Not yet the devil from later Christian thinking, the snake is simply one of God's creatures who brings chaos and bewilderment into the Garden. Unique about him is his "cunning," his cleverness (3:1). Besides telling us about the snake's character, the word "cunning" (*arum*) is important at another level. The narrator chooses a Hebrew word (*arum*) that resembles the word translated "naked" (*arummim*) in the previous verse (2:25). The wordplay between "cunning" and "nakedness" is itself cunning for it points ahead in the story to the couple's nakedness (*arummim*, v. 7). It is the snake's cunning, his clever slyness, that deceives them and changes the way they understand their nakedness (3:7).

The snake talks with the woman about God's command not to eat from the trees in the middle of the Garden, but the snake's opening words are cunningly inaccurate. Making a specific taboo into a general one, the snake asks if God has forbidden them from eating of "any of the trees of the garden" (v. 1) rather than only of the two in the middle of the Garden (2:15). The woman quickly corrects him, but she, too, alters God's prohibition by adding to it: "Only the fruit of the tree of the middle of the garden" was forbidden to them, she replies. But she adds a new detail to God's command. "You may not touch it, or else you will die" (v. 3). God never mentioned touching the tree (2:16). Perhaps, as Phyllis Trible suggested, the woman was putting another prohibition around the main one to create a barrier in advance of the act of eating the fruit to put another step between her and eating.

The snake undermines trust in God's words even further by blatantly contradicting them. "[If you eat from the tree], you will certainly not die." In fact, eating it will open her eyes, he claims, and "you will be like gods who know good and evil" (v. 5). This story of the cunning snake is itself cunning because the snake turns out to be correct. When the couple eats from the tree, they do not die and they do learn that the world is a place of good and evil. Eating opens their eyes to reality. The wily snake persuades the woman to look closely at the tree and see the possible benefits of eating from it. In the forbidden tree, she sees what God had said earlier about the other trees in the Garden (3:6; cf. 2:9). The tree was "good for food and pleasing to the eyes," but now the snake suggests something more: "The tree was desirable for gaining wisdom" (3:6).

The value of the tree—its beauty and productiveness, its capacity to open eyes and produce wisdom—makes it irresistible. Are these not what most people want? The woman takes the fruit, eats it, and shares it with "her man" who "was with her." He has been with her through the whole conversation with the snake, and he eats it, too. And just as the snake promised, their eyes are opened, and they know they are naked. To have open eyes in this story means that they discover their shame. Shame creeps into knowledge of their bodies, disturbs the relationship of each within themselves, and degrades their mutual connection. In the first cover-up, they cover up their bodies with fig leaves.

Hiding (3:8–13)

The idyllic life of the first act (2:4–25) continues to unravel as the effects of eating of the fruit become clear. In a shift from narrative to conversation, these verses convey the severing of relationships that previously seemed secure. When God walks in the Garden, the man and the woman hear him, and they hide. Now, besides feeling shame, they also feel fear. Fear keeps them from going forward openly and truthfully to meet God, and it is fear that leads to the next cover-up. God takes the initiative and calls to the man with a question that resounds through the ages: "Where are you?" (v. 9). Notice that God is not portrayed as omniscient, enabling God to ask of the human a question that seems more than geographical in intent. Not only "Where are you hiding?" but "What are you hiding?" and "Why are you hiding?" are implied.

The man steps out and admits his fear. Note the first-person speech: "I heard you in the garden; but I was afraid, because I was naked, so I hid" (v.10). Adam limits his concern to "I," not "we," suggesting a crack in his relationship with the woman. As the dialogue continues, God wants to know who told him he was naked. "Have you eaten from the tree of which I had forbidden you to eat?" (v. 11).

Adam's speech with its "I" language may point to a strain in the couple's relationship, but when they speak with God their harmonious connection breaks down even more. No longer does the man sing of the union of their bones and flesh; instead, he blames her for their problem and then blames God for giving her to him. "The woman whom you put here with me—she gave me the fruit from the tree, so I ate it" (3:12). Angry, defensive, and accusatory, Adam refuses to take responsibility for what he has done. But the woman is no better than he. When God asks her, "What is this you have done?" she responds just like her man. "The snake tricked me so I ate it" (v. 13). She too tries to cover up her involvement, refuses to take responsibility for her actions, and blames the snake for tricking her. The domestic bliss of the couple disappears in mutual recrimination. The humans lie about their role in eating the fruit; they blame others, they separate from each other, and even drive a wedge between themselves and the animals in the form of the snake.

The second act of the dramatic story depicts the falling apart of the world. After the disclosure of human disobedience, the prose of the narrator gives way to poetry where God decrees punishments to each of the characters. Each punishment explains why things are the way they are.

Poetry of Punishment (3:14–19)

The snake, the woman, the ground, and the man all receive punishments from God in this poetry. The snake and the ground are objects of curses. Curses predict disaster, and in this case, because the curses come from God they have added power. But the humans are merely punished, not cursed. In this story, disobedience provokes punishments from God that alter relationships in creation and disrupt life in Eden's paradise. Disobedience explains why the world is broken.

Disobedience is the reason that snakes have no legs and slide on their bellies. God addresses the snake directly: "Because you have done this, cursed are you among all the animals" (v. 14). The curse makes the snake into the creature we know a snake to be, one that crawls and slithers and creates fear among humans. The snake will be "at enmity" or at war with the woman, and that warfare will extend to all the offspring of humans and snakes. The humans will try to cut off snakes' heads, and the snakes will try to bite the humans' heels. The peaceful relationship in chapter 2 where the man names animals and where animals and humans are created from the same ground now erupts into a permanent state of conflict.

Catholic devotion will later find in verse 15 the basis for the famous depiction of Mary crushing the head of the serpent with her heel. It is Mary's Son, her offspring Jesus, who will crush the power of Satan. But in Genesis the text tells of strife between humans and animals caused by their complicity in disobeying God.

Disobedience is the reason that women suffer in their roles as mothers and wives. The woman's punishment affects her sexually determined roles in the ancient world (v. 16). Her pain in childbearing will be intensified (did it already exist?), and her yearning for her man will not be satisfied by mutual, reverent love. She will, instead, be subjected to him, his desires and whims, while he will rule her. Of the two humans, she receives the shorter punishment, not because it is the mildest but because in the ancient world, women were not judged to be equal to men. The world revolved around men, and women were generally subordinate to them. The story both reflects and enacts that ancient reality. But here, at least, women's subordination is clearly the consequence of disobedience, not the original plan of God in creating the couple in the Garden.

Disobedience is the reason that men labor in the fields by the sweat of their brows and why the ground resists their efforts (vv. 17–19). God reminds

Adam of the prohibition against eating from the tree and then reinforces the couple's broken relationship. "Because you listened" to her, "cursed is the ground because of you" (v. 17). Disharmony already present between the man and woman now extends between humans and the ground. The curse of the ground places the responsibility for it upon Adam's shoulders. The ground is no longer the productive, fertile oasis of Eden, filled with ripe trees; now it yields thorns and thistles and grass. Although the ground does not return to the barren desert of the opening verses (2:4–5), it produces little to eat of its own accord.

The man's punishment arises from his role as the tiller of the ground, the agricultural labors that God assigned to him in the Garden. Although he rules over his wife and she must yield to his control, over the ground he has no control. Only by the sweat of his brow, by intense physical labor, will the ground yield food for him until he returns to the ground itself. "For you are dust and to dust you shall return" (3:19). In a circle looping back to human origins from the dust of the ground, the human will return again to the ground from which he was taken. He is mortal now and will become dust again, as Catholics and other Christians recall on Ash Wednesday. The snake was right. Humans do not die immediately after eating the fruit, but they will. God does not condemn the man to death. He and the woman bring mortality upon themselves by eating the forbidden fruit.

The man and the woman, the snake and the ground each have distinctive roles in the story, but each too, also stands for the whole of their species. The snake is among the animals, "tame and wild," and represents them all. The woman and her offspring, male and female, will be at odds with the snake and other animals. The man labors in the fields in order to eat, but his work is onerous and unrewarding, requiring all his strength. All creation remains interconnected in the second act, but the bonds of unity, trust, and peace disappear in the midst of pain, alienation, and conflict. And death awaits all.

These punishments and this entire story provide reasons why things are as they are. Interpreters call these types of stories "etiologies." Disobedience to God's commands created a broken world. Humans listened to the snake, twisted God's words, ate from the forbidden tree, hid from God, denied responsibility for their actions, and undermined their connections to one another. Yet so far the text never uses any vocabulary of sin. Hebrew has at least three different terms for sin, but none occur here. Why not? Language of sin enters the Bible in the next chapter when Cain murders his brother Abel (4:1–16). There, blood violence is sin, refusing to be one another's keeper is sin. There, sin is a force waiting to pounce on Cain, and he does not resist it. Why does the Garden story not speak about sin but only imply the sinfulness of disobeying God's word?

The Garden story seems less interested in presenting a doctrine of human sinfulness than in an account of how things differ from God's plan for mutual respect, interaction, and harmony within the created world. Human irresponsibility is the source of the world's brokenness, but human failure arises in conjunction with the cleverness of the snake, one among God's creatures. Does the story suggest there is a fundamental flaw in creation itself that such a creature might engage the humans against the divine command? Does it start from the reality of brokenness and then work backward to imagine an explanation? Or does it teach about sin indirectly, precisely to encourage questions from readers about the realities in which we live?

Expulsion (3:20–24)

In the final scene, the narrator resumes speaking in the drama's sequel. First, Adam uses another wordplay to name the woman that arises from her role as "the mother of all the living" (v. 20). In Hebrew the name "Eve" resembles the verb "to live." Eve's name honors her as mother of new life, the source of all humanity, yet she diminishes in importance, subject as she is to the domination of her man in both the text and in this broken world.

Next the narrator informs us that God does not abandon the couple. The story is not a tragedy because it ends with hope. Despite their disobedience, God makes clothes for Adam and Eve from the skins of animals. The clothes provide warmth, protection from the elements, and they hide the shame they now feel for their bodies. This small narrative detail reveals divine care for creation and shows that God does not abandon them as they leave the Garden.

Yet something else is amiss. When God speaks to an unnamed group using first-person plural language, God seems afraid of human power: "The man has become like one of us, knowing good from evil!" (3:22). The plural "us" may be conventional royal speech, spoken by an individual to emphasize authority, or more likely, God may be addressing the heavenly court of angelic or semi-divine beings (see Gen 1:26; 11:7). But to whomever God refers, fear of the human emerges, as if knowing good and evil made Adam equal to God. Perhaps in this story God worries that Adam's abandonment of innocent childhood in the Garden will also give him courage and the freedom to "take fruit from the tree of life," and then to live forever (v. 23). To remain ignorant will leave the couple like children but to know and become adult requires that they disobey God.

Knowing good from evil is one thing, but even more serious is the possibility that the humans might eat from the tree of life. Immortality is the true danger here, for, in the terms of this story, it would make humans like God. To prevent access to the tree of life, God banishes Adam from the Garden "to till the ground from which he had been taken" (v. 23) and then posts a cherubim with a flaming sword at the Garden's entrance. Humans cannot gain access to the tree of life and without it they will die. This story struggles with the question of why humans die, and it concludes that humans, in collusion with the snake, bring it upon themselves, yet God plays a part as well, for God bars their way to the tree. Immortality is forever walled off from them by the cherubim with a flaming sword. This is the way it is; we return to dust.

CONCLUSION

Whereas a major theme of the story's first act (2:4–25), the point toward which it drives, is the creation and celebration of sexuality, the major theme of the second act is loss of immortality. But underlying these themes is a larger set of issues. The story imagines a perfect world in act 1, but in act 2, all the relationships of harmony, interconnectedness, and well-being fracture and disintegrate. God's plan for the world breaks down because the snake and the humans do not accept their limits, do not obey the restrictions placed upon them in that agreeable green Garden. This creation account presents life and death, the first as a gift of God and the second as the result of divine resistance against human encroachment into the heavenly realm. We can see how a doctrine of original sin finds a basis in the story.

To read the Genesis story carefully rather than just receiving it as a simple account of the first sin is to confront questions about its purposes. Is this a story about reality and how it came to be? Does it not contain insight into the way life is mired in conflicts, where humans live with inner shame and lie to cover up their disobedience and where the love of a couple turns to blaming, where hiding from God seems self-protective, and where work can be hard, thankless, and unproductive?

In this story human life appears the way it is. Humans seek those things that are good to the eye and give wisdom and knowledge of good and evil. It is peculiar that the Hebrew never uses any of its rich vocabulary for sin. Genesis reserves sin language for the murder and sees it as a force lurking to prey upon Cain who cannot master it (Gen 4).

The Garden story is told with subtle irony, slippery like the snake. The humans emerge from innocent ignorance of childhood to know the reality of good and evil. They see the world as it is and begin to enact the dissonance, brokenness, and shamefulness of that reality. They do not die, but in another twist, they are barred from immortal life by the fiery sword of an angel and live with the unfathomable reality of death, their own, each other's and of all living things. Yet God prepares them for that world by covering them with clothes as they walk out of the Garden into reality. The story tells the truth and holds up a mirror of our world.

QUESTIONS

1. Why does the woman eat the fruit? What does she desire that eating it will seem to fill? What would you do in her position?

2. What do you think is the main thrust of the two chapters together?

3. Do the beautiful world and the broken world exist in the present?

4. Trace what God does from scene to scene in the story. Does a pattern emerge?

5. What incidents in your life arise as you read this story? What does God do in your life and your community to protect and guide?

BIBLIOGRAPHY

Cotter, David W. *Genesis*. Berit OSeries. Collegeville, MN: Liturgical Press, 2003.

LaCoque, André. *The Trial of Innocence: Adam, Eve, and the Yahwist*. Eugene, OR: Cascade, 2006.

Sharp, Carolyn J. *Irony and Meaning in the Hebrew Bible*. Bloomington, IN: Indiana University Press, 2009, especially pp. 35–42.

Trible, Phyllis. *God and the Rhetoric of Sexuality*. Philadelphia: Fortress Press, 1978.

Chapter 3

WHY READ ANCIENT MESOPOTAMIAN STORIES?

Roberta Salvador, MM

READ GENESIS 1:1—2:25; GENESIS 6–9; EXODUS 1:22—2:10; GENESIS 37:39–45

INTRODUCTION: ANCIENT MESOPOTAMIAN STORIES

The name "Mesopotamia" comes from two Greek words: *mesos*, meaning "middle," and *potamos*, meaning "river." As its name suggests, Mesopotamia refers to the land between two rivers, the Tigris and Euphrates. In ancient times, Mesopotamia included Assyria, Babylonia, and Sumer. Today it is modern Iraq and eastern Syria that lie in the same area (see Collins). Historians believe farmers and fishermen were settled in Mesopotamia as early as 5500 BC.

Sumerian cuneiform was one of the earliest writing systems. Cuneiform was written with a stylus or reed pen pressed to make wedges on clay tablets. The tablets were dried in the sun or baked. This is one of the reasons poems, stories, law codes, treaties, and letters have survived over thousands of years. These tablets were stored in the temples and royal palaces. Much of the literature of ancient Mesopotamia has come down to us in Akkadian, the language spoken in Babylonia and Assyria from about 2500 BC.

Why is Mesopotamian literature significant to the study of the Hebrew Bible or Old Testament? Mesopotamia was not only the geographical setting of the literature of the ancient Near Eastern world; it was also the cultural matrix for much of its literature. We find the influence of ancient Near Eastern literature in the biblical texts. Thus, we find many parallels between ancient Mesopotamian myths, stories, poems, and wisdom sayings and those of the Hebrew Bible:

- Ancient Mesopotamia had its creation and flood stories. The *Enuma Elish* is the Babylonian creation story. The Epic of Atrahasis tells the story of a great flood. Like Noah, King Atrahasis follows divine advice (in this case, from the god Enki), builds an ark, gathers his family, animals, and birds onto the ark, and waits out the flood aboard it while humanity is devastated. As in the story of Gilgamesh, an epic poem about the partially divine king of Uruk, Noah offers sacrifice as soon as he touches dry land once again.
- Sargon of Agade (or Akkad), son of a high priestess, is hidden in a reed basket by the river, as was Moses.
- The importance of clothes as a symbol of identity, function, and status runs through the stories of Joseph and his brothers, and can be compared to the symbolic value of clothes in the story of the goddess Ishtar's descent into the netherworld.
- The biblical Job and the figure in the lengthy Babylonian poetic monologue Poem of the Righteous Sufferer both lose their fortunes, health, and standing in the community only to regain them in the end.
- There are Hebrew proverbs and wise sayings that are similar to those of ancient Mesopotamia.

This essay compares some of the literary pieces mentioned above with stories in the books of Genesis and Exodus. We will start with the creation story.

THE EPIC OF CREATION—THE *ENUMA ELISH* (READ GENESIS 1:1—2:25)

The *Enuma Elish* is the Babylonian creation epic. Its title comes from the opening lines of the story, "When on high." It is written in Akkadian, the language of ancient Babylon, in poetic form, on seven tablets. The date of its composition is uncertain, although some scholars believe that its language and content place it in the latter half of the second millennium BC. The theme of the story is how the god Marduk fights and wins the battle against a goddess, Tiamat, who is joined by the forces of chaos. After the battle, the gods build Esagila, Marduk's temple in Babylon, and acclaim Marduk as their leader and head. The epic ends with an acclamation of Marduk's many exalted titles and description of all his glorious accomplishments. Some scholars believe the *Enuma Elish* may have been recited at the spring festival, the Akitu festival, which began the agricultural year. The festival celebrated the triumph of order over chaos and the renewal of the earth. Let us now look at the story.

The *Enuma Elish* begins at a time before there was a heaven, earth, and a pantheon of gods. There exist only two primordial waters, the sweet, fresh water below the earth, personified as the god Apsu, and ocean or salt water, personified as the goddess Tiamat (also called Mummu-Tiamat). Creation begins with the begetting of the gods. Apsu and Tiamat commingle to give birth to the gods.

> When on high the heaven had not been named,
> Firm ground below had not been called by name,
> Naught but primordial Apsu, their begetter,
> (And) Mummu-Tiamat, she who bore them all,
> Their waters commingling as a single body;
> No reed hut had been matted, no marsh land had appeared,
> When no gods whatever had been brought into being,
> Uncalled by name, their destinies undetermined—
> Then it was that the gods were formed within them.
> (*ANET*, Tablet I, 1–9)

The story continues with the birth of other gods, Lahmu and Lahamu, Anshar and Kishar, who are the circle or horizon of heaven and earth. Anu is the god of heaven and Ea the god of wisdom. But the young gods are so noisy that they disturb Apsu, who complains he cannot sleep day or night. Apsu and Mummu-Tiamat conspire to destroy the young gods. However, the young gods find out about the plot and rebel. They choose Marduk to lead the uprising.

Marduk is described as having four eyes that see everything, four ears that are enormous, and lips that blaze forth fire. The description continues:

> He was the loftiest of the gods, surpassing was his stature;
> His members were enormous, he was exceeding tall....
> Clothed with the halo of ten gods, he was strong to the utmost
> (*ANET*, Tablet I, 99–103)

Marduk challenges Tiamat to meet in single combat. He spreads his net over Tiamat and blows the fierce winds on her face. Tiamat swallows the winds, which distend her belly. Marduk shoots an arrow, which pierces her belly and splits her heart. He then splits her down the middle and kills her. Marduk throws down her corpse and slices her "in half like a fish for drying."

Half of her body he throws up to make the sky. With the other half, he makes the earth.

Marduk places the other gods into the sky as constellations, which mark the months and days of the year. In Tiamat's belly, Marduk locates the zenith. He makes the moon and entrusts night to it. He assigns this creature of the night to mark out the days, "monthly, without cease…at the month's very start, rising over the land." He tells the moon that when Shamash, the sun, rises in the horizon, then the moon should shed its "crown," or visibility, and begin to wane. The moon delegates the days of the month, while the sun is responsible for the year. Marduk opens up springs, the Euphrates and the Tigris, from Tiamat's eyes. He then designates the cult and creates its rites, while the gods look on with joy.

It is not clear whether the authors of the creation stories in Genesis knew about the *Enuma Elish*. Certainly the *Enuma Elish* predates Genesis. Some scholars believe there are enough parallels with the Mesopotamian story that the author of Genesis 1:1—2:3 may have known about it. Or, as others have surmised, perhaps the parallels may have come simply from universal themes in creation stories among different ethnic groups. However, there are enough similarities to pose the question, what are some of the similarities and differences?

Both the *Enuma Elish* and Genesis stories begin with watery chaos. In the *Enuma Elish* chaos takes the form of a commingling of primordial salty and fresh waters, "Two bodies of water becoming one." There is nothing before the waters. In the Genesis story there is also "a formless void," which indicates a chaotic formlessness, associated with the waters of "the deep." In the *Enuma Elish* the heavens and earth come into existence out of this chaos because of a conflict among the gods and the single combat between Marduk and Tiamat. Marduk makes the heavens from half of the defeated Tiamat's body, and the earth from the other half. In Genesis, on the other hand, the world comes into being because God speaks: "Let there be light…. Let there be a dome….Let the dry land appear….Let there be lights in the dome of the sky….Let the waters bring forth swarms of living creatures, and let birds fly above the earth across the dome of the sky…; let the earth bring forth living creatures of every kind: cattle and creeping things and wild animals of the earth of every kind." The biblical God creates light, the heavens, the heavenly bodies, and all the animals by the power of the divine word.

In the *Enuma Elish*, the Mesopotamian gods do not create light but are themselves luminous. This is how Marduk is described: "'My son, the sun! sunlight of the gods!' He wore [on his body] the auras of ten gods, had [them] wrapped around his head too" (*ANET*, Tablet I, 102–3). When Tiamat assembles her army, consisting of fierce dragons and monster serpents, she causes them "to bear auras like gods" (*ANET*, Tablet II, 4). Marduk creates the constellations of stars by positioning the great gods in the heavens, and using them to mark the year and days of the year (*ANET*, Tablet V, 2–4). The God of the Bible creates the luminaries to be the signs and seasons for days and years, and to give light upon the earth.

Where Marduk makes the earth from half of Tiamat's body, the biblical God creates the earth by separating the dry land from the waters of the sea. God separates the waters above the firmament, or dome, from the waters below, and then gathers the waters below in one place so that dry land appears and plants can grow. God then tells the waters to bring forth fish and sea creatures. On the sixth day of creation, God orders the earth to bring forth animals and the first man and woman. In the *Enuma Elish* there is no description of the creation of the creatures of the sea, sky, and land. Marduk makes human beings so that they should do the work of the gods and the gods can have leisure. Here is Marduk speaking:

> Blood I will mass and cause bone to be.
> I will establish a savage, "man" shall be his name.
> Verily, savage-man I will create.
> He shall be charged with the service of the god
> That they might be at ease! (*ANET*, Tablet VI, 5–8)

The gods tie up the god, Kingu, Tiamat's commander-in-chief. Ea slits his throat, and from his blood the gods fashion humankind. In contrast to the violent beginning of humankind in the *Enuma Elish*, the God of Genesis tells the story of a blessed beginning. God creates the man and woman in his own image, blesses them, and tells them to "be fruitful and multiply, and fill the earth." It is a blessed beginning. In fact, the Genesis story makes the point that God sees each work of creation and all creatures as "good" and blesses them.

THE STORY OF THE GREAT FLOOD AND
THE EPIC OF ATRAHASIS (READ GENESIS 6–9)

The Epic of Atrahasis is of interest to students of the Bible because of parallels with the flood and Noah stories (Gen 6–8). According to Dalley, the name "Atrahasis" means "Extra-wise." An Assyrian version was found in the palace of King Ashurbanipal, the last of the great kings of the Assyrian Empire, who reigned in the seventh century BC.

Atrahasis is the story of the creation of humankind, which includes within it a story of a flood. The story opens with the gods digging watercourses.

> When the gods instead of man
> Did the work, bore the loads,

The gods' load was too great,
The work too hard, the trouble too much. (*Myths*, Tablet I, 1–4)

After years of drudgery, the gods tire of working and decide to create humans to do their work for them. They fashion humankind by killing Aw-ilu, one of the gods, and mixing clay with his flesh and blood. But in time the humans become so noisy that they disturb the gods. Enlil, head of the pantheon, gets angry because he cannot sleep. He orders a drought and food to be cut off. As the drought progresses, the people get so hungry that mothers and daughters are sold as slaves, and daughters and sons are eaten for food. The gods then send a pestilence. But the people are not diminished and remain as numerous as before. The divine assembly then decides to send a flood that will wipe out humanity.

The gods warn Enki not to tell his friend King Atrahasis of their plans. However, when Atrahasis falls asleep in Enki's temple, he begins to dream. He asks Enki to tell him the message of the dream. Because he has promised the other gods not to tell Atrahasis how to escape the flood, Enki does not speak directly to Atrahasis, but to a wall. Enki tells the wall—that is, Atrahasis, who is listening—to leave his house and possessions, build a boat, put a roof over it, and cover it with pitch, for he was going to send a seven-day deluge.

> Wall, listen constantly to me!
> Reed hut, make sure you attend to all my words!
> Dismantle the house, build a boat,
> Reject possessions, and save living things.
> The boat that you build…
> Roof it like the Apsu
> So that the Sun cannot see inside it!
> Make upper decks and lower decks.
> The tackle must be very strong,
> The bitumen strong, to give strength.
> I shall make rain fall on you here. (*Myths*, Tablet III, i, 20–33)

Atrahasis calls together some elders, a carpenter with an axe, a reed-worker to carry stone, a rich man to carry the pitch, and a poor man to bring the materials needed. They begin to build the boat. Atrahasis slaughters cattle, sheep, and birds for food. He brings these and live animals on the boat. He then brings his family on board. Atrahasis seals the door with pitch. The storm begins. Atrahasis cuts the mooring rope and releases the boat.

The gods, who now have no food and drink because there are no humans to offer sacrifice of food and drink to them, regret their decision. But there is nothing they can do, for the flood covers the earth for seven days and seven nights. The cuneiform text is broken at this point. It is assumed that the flood eventually subsides. Another story of a flood, which is told within the epic poem about Gilgamesh, completes the ending. When the land dries, Utnapishtim, who tells Gilgamesh the story, offers a sacrifice to the gods.

The biblical story of the flood has similarities to and differences from the Atrahasis story. Atrahasis and Noah are both extraordinary men. Interestingly, they both are close to their gods.

> Now there was one Atrahasis
> Whose ear was open (to) his god Enki.
> He would speak with his god
> And his god would speak with him.
> Atrahasis made his voice heard
> And spoke to his lord. (*Myths*, Tablet I, vii)

Here is how Noah is described, "Noah was a righteous man, blameless in his generation; Noah walked with God" (Gen 6:9). In both stories, the deities send the rains because they are displeased with humankind. The gods choose Atrahasis and Noah to warn of the coming destruction. The god Enki gives Atrahasis specifications about how he should build the boat.

> The barge should be....
> Place a roof over it,
>   Cover it like Apsu, The Heavens, covers The Earth.
> Do not let The Sun see inside,
>   Enclose it completely.
> Make the joints strong,
> Caulk the timers with pitch. (*Old Testament Parallels*, Tablet III,
>   7–35)

Similarly, God tells Noah how to build the ark: "Make yourself an ark of cypress wood...and cover it inside and out with pitch....Make a roof for the ark, and finish it to a cubit above; and put the door of the ark in its side; make it with lower, second, and third decks" (Gen 6:14–16). In the Babylonian story, Enki tells Atrahasis he will provide him with food: "I will shower down upon you later /A windfall of birds, a spate of fishes" (Tablet III, 34–35). On the other hand, the biblical God tells Noah to take food with him, "Also take with you every kind of food that is eaten, and store it up; and it shall serve as food for you and for them [Noah's wife, sons and their wives]" (Gen 6:21). God instructs Noah, telling him how many clean and unclean animals and birds he should take "to keep them alive" (Gen 6:20). Genesis recounts how the rain fell for forty days and forty nights, a way of saying that it rained for a very long time. The flood stays on the earth at least forty days (or a hundred and fifty, in Genesis 7:24).

The Atrahasis story describes the flood in dramatic detail:

> The flood rushed forward,
>> The flood charged the people like an army.
> One person could not see the other,
>> In the water no one was recognizable.
> The flood bellowed like a bull,
>> The winds howled like a wild ass braying....
> There was no sun,
> Only the darkness of the flood. (*Old Testament Parallels*,
>> Tablet III, 12–20)

In Atrahasis the flood covers the earth for seven days and seven nights, annihilating the people, terrifying the gods, and making them repent their deeds, because there are no longer any humans to work for them. Here the tablet breaks off and the story is unfinished. The Babylonian epic poem about Gilgamesh, continues the story. After the waters subside, Utnapishtim, who tells the story of the flood, leaves the ark, builds an altar, and offers sacrifice. "The gods smelled the aroma/They swarmed like flies around his sacrifice" (Tablet III, 35–36). Like Utnapishtim, Noah builds an altar to the Lord, takes the clean animals and birds, and offers them as burnt offerings. The Lord smells the burnt offerings and promises never to destroy humankind again (Gen 8:20–22).

THE BIRTHS OF MOSES AND SARGON OF AKKAD
(READ EXODUS 1:22—2:10)

Akkad was one of the great cities of the ancient world. King Sargon, who ruled Akkad, was reputed to have founded the first empire in history. According to Sargon's own account, he was placed in a reed basket as a baby and hidden in the river. The river carries the basket to Aqqi, "drawer of water," a gardener, who adopts him. Sargon works in Aqqi's orchard, but grows up to become king. He attributes his good fortune to Ishtar, Babylonian goddess of love and fertility. Below is the beginning of the Sargon text.

> I am Sargon the great king, king of Agade
> My mother was a high priestess, I did not know my father.
> My father's brothers dwell in the uplands.
> My city is Azupiranu, which lies on Euphrates bank.

My mother, the high priestess, conceived me, she bore me in secret.
She placed me in a reed basket, she sealed my hatch with pitch.
She left me to the river, whence I could not come up.
The river carried me off, it brought me to Aqqi, drawer of water,
Aqqi, drawer of water, brought me up as he dipped his bucket.
Aqqi, drawer of water, raised me as his adopted son.
Aqqi, drawer of water, set (me) to his orchard work.
During my orchard work, Ishtar loved me,
Fifty-five years I ruled as king.
I became lord over and ruled the black-headed folk.
I ...[ ] hard mountains with picks of copper,
I was wont to ascend high mountains,
I was wont to cross low mountains.
The [l]and of the sea I sieged three times, I conquered Dilmun.
I went up to great Der, I [ ],
I destroyed [Ka]zallu and [ ].... (*From Distant Days*, II, 1–20)

The stories of Moses and Sargon bear remarkable similarities to one another. At the time Moses is born, the king of Egypt has mandated that all sons born to Hebrew women should be cast into the Nile and killed. But Moses' mother puts him in a basket made of bulrushes and hides him among the reeds at the river's bank. Pharoah's daughter comes down to the river to bathe and finds the baby. She takes the baby and has his mother nurse him. Moses is considered the son of Pharaoh's daughter and has a privileged social status. When Moses grows up, he takes pity on the Hebrews and leads them out of Egypt into freedom.

Although Sargon is raised by a "drawer of water" and is taught to tend orchards, he is highborn, the son of a high priestess. Moses, like Sargon, is also born from the priestly class, his mother and father being from the house of Levi, and he marries a wife whose father is a priest of Midian. Both Sargon and Moses are hidden by their mothers because their births must be kept a secret. Both are placed in baskets as infants and placed near water. Sargon's basket floats down the river and is picked up by a gardener, who raises him in humble circumstances. Moses' basket is found by Pharaoh's daughter, although he is raised by his own mother, also in humble circumstances. Sargon believes he is especially protected and loved by the goddess Ishtar, becomes king, and proudly accomplishes great feats over a long reign. Moses is chosen by the God of the Hebrews for a special mission. He confronts Pharaoh, delivers the people from bondage, makes a covenant with the Lord, and receives the law from God in a face-to-face meeting on the holy mountain of Sinai. Both fulfill their destinies of being leaders of their people.

CLOTHING IN THE STORIES OF JOSEPH AND HIS BROTHERS AND ISHTAR'S DESCENT TO THE NETHERWORLD (READ GENESIS 37:39–45)

Clothes play a significant part in the Babylonian story the Descent of Ishtar to the Netherworld. Ishtar, the goddess of fertility and love, goes to the netherworld to visit Ereshkigal, Queen of the netherworld. To do so, she must pass through seven gates. At each gate, the gatekeeper demands a piece of her clothing. At the first gate, he takes the great crown on her head.

> Then the first door he had made her enter,
> He stripped and took away the great crown on her head.
> "Why, O gatekeeper, didst thou take the great crown on my head?"
> "Enter, my lady, thus are the rules of the Mistress of the Nether
>   World." (*ANET*, II, 42–45)

At the second gate, the gatekeeper takes away the pendants on her ears.

> When the second gate he had made her enter,
> He stripped and took away the pendants on her ears.
> "Why, O gatekeeper, didst thou take the pendants on my ears?"
> "Enter, my lady, thus are the rules of the Mistress of the Nether
>   World." (*ANET*, II, 46–49)

At the third gate, he takes away the chains around her neck; at the fourth gate, the ornaments on her breast; at the fifth gate, the girdle of birthstones on her hips; at the sixth gate, the clasps round her hands and feet; and at the seventh gate, the breechcloth on her body. When she reaches the netherworld, Ishtar no longer has any of her regal clothing or sign of her status as goddess. Moreover, Ereshkigal sends sixty illnesses against her. When Ishtar becomes powerless and without any of the signs that identify her, all fertility stops on the earth above.

> The bull springs not upon the cow, [the ass impregnates not the
>   jenny],
> In the street [the man impregnates not] the maiden.
> The man lies [in his (own) chamber, the maiden lies on her side].
>   (*ANET*, II, 77–79)

Papsukkal, vizier of the gods, becomes worried and goes to Ea, the high god. Ea sends the eunuch Asushunamir to bring Ishtar back from the Netherworld. Eventually, Namtar, Ereshkigal's vizier, brings Ishtar successively through the seven gates. At the first gate, he returns the breechcloth for her body. At the second gate, he returns the clasps for her hands and feet, and so forth at each gate, until the last gate when he returns the great crown for her head. As the clothes that signify Ishtar's status and function as the goddess of love and fertility are returned to her, love and fertility return to the earth above.

In the biblical story of Joseph, as in the Babylonian story of Ishtar, clothes play a major part. Jacob loved Joseph the best of his sons, "because he was the son of his old age" (Gen 37:3), and unwisely made him a long tunic, a garment totally unsuited for working in the fields. When he receives news of Joseph's death, Jacob tears his clothes in mourning. Joseph is sold to Potiphar, a chief steward in Pharoah's court. When Potiphar's wife tries to get Joseph to sleep with her, Joseph refuses, but she grabs his cloak, turns the story around, and shows Potiphar Joseph's cloak as proof. Joseph saves Egypt during the time of famine by interpreting Pharaoh's dreams. In gratitude, he is given a signet ring, fine linen robes, and a gold chain, signs of his new office, and his new higher status as Pharaoh's favor. In Egypt, the brothers tear their clothes in mourning when Joseph's servants find the missing silver cup in Benjamin's sack. At the resolution of the story, Joseph gives his brothers food and sets of clothes, a sign that he has forgiven them, that he holds no grudge, and that he has restored them to their former status.

In both stories clothes signify the person's status in the family and society. Status is connected not only to the person's standing, but also to his or her identity. Ishtar's great crown, robes, pendant, jewels, and belt identify her as an important goddess. Without these outward signs, she no longer functions as goddess of fertility and love. It is interesting that in the Joseph story, there is also much made of clothes, emphasizing the symbolic value of clothes in the story. Joseph's long tunic with the long sleeves marks him as the favored son. When he is made governor over the land of Egypt, he is given the clothes and ring appropriate to the office.

CONCLUSION

There are other texts from Mesopotamia that are similar in form and content to those in the Hebrew Bible. The biblical Job reminds us of the Righteous Sufferer in the Babylonian poem. There are Babylonian lamentations and elegies like those in the Hebrew Bible. The Neo-Babylonian Lament for Tammuz is a lament in which the grieving women of Uruk and Addak weep over their dead husbands and the devastation of Ur, much like Ishtar grieved and wept over her consort, Tammuz. That lament and the Lamentation over the Destruction of Ur over the destruction of a city are reminiscent of the Book of Lamentations:

O city, a bitter lament set up as thy lament;
His righteous city which has been destroyed—bitter is its lament;
His Ur which has been destroyed—bitter is its lament.
(*ANET*, 456)

The lament Against Enlil's Anger begins "How long, O Lord, how long? Help me!" (*ANET*, 560), like the plaintive cries of the psalmist in Psalms 13:1, 2; 89:46; and 79:5. There are Babylonian hymns on the occasion of the king's coronation, the king's illness, or the king's victories that can be compared to some of the royal hymns of the Book of Psalms. The various sections in the Prayers to Marduk that seek protection against the deity's anger, against illness, and against impending evil are similar to the petitionary prayers of the psalms. The Shamash Hymn and the great creation psalm, Psalm 104, both speak of the greatness of the deity who illuminates the heavens and provides for the creatures of the earth. The Code of Hammurabi has been compared to some of the legal texts in Exodus, Numbers, and Deuteronomy. The Sumerian courtly love song the Faithful Lover, as well as other love songs, has been compared to the biblical Song of Songs. There are Hebrew proverbs and sayings that are reminiscent of Babylonian wisdom literature. Perhaps the value of becoming acquainted with the Mesopotamian texts lies in heightening our awareness of the cultural matrix for some of the stories and literature of the Hebrew Bible.

QUESTIONS

1. What picture of God do you get in Genesis? How is that impression similar or different from the picture of the gods of the Babylonian pantheon, especially of the god Marduk? Marduk is head of the pantheon. If you were an ancient Babylonian, would you have felt comfortable praying to him for help in your troubles? Explain your position.

2. Atrahasis, like the biblical Noah, is especially singled out by the gods. They foreordain that he will be saved, while the rest of humanity is destroyed in the flood. Do you believe that some people are especially chosen by God to perform a special task? Give examples of "chosen" people in our age. What qualities mark them as special or remarkable? Would you consider such characteristics a blessing from God, or something they achieved through their own efforts? Do you think God brings about natural disasters, like tsunamis, fires, or earthquakes, in order to teach human beings a lesson?

3. King Sargon of Akkad and Moses both are hidden by their mothers as newly born infants. Their lives have precarious beginnings. Do you think children who are born and grow up in difficult environments can grow up to become self-assured, confident, productive, and "good" people; or must they

necessarily be thwarted by their early difficulties? Give reasons or examples for the side you take.

4. Joseph was the favorite of his father. Do parents generally have favorites even though they may claim to love their children equally? *Can* parents love their children equally, or is that an unrealistic expectation? Were Joseph's brothers "evil" for feeling jealous toward Joseph, or was jealous a natural feeling, considering the circumstances? Can you think of an instance when you had to work hard at overcoming a terrible dislike for a person, or a feeling you consider negative and harmful to yourself? How were you able to overcome such a feeling? Is the Joseph character realistic or unrealistic for not wreaking vengeance on his brothers when he had the upper hand?

5. In the stories of Joseph and the Descent of Ishtar to the Netherworld, clothes have a significant symbolic value. In our everyday lives, what role do clothes play? Do they contribute to the value people give to other people? What other things contribute to give people a sense of who they are? What things, in your opinion, best define the status, identity, and worth of a person?

6. The peoples of ancient Mesopotamia wondered about the world they lived in and composed stories to answer their questions. The peoples of ancient Israel did likewise. Why are those of ancient Israel considered "Sacred Scripture," whereas those of ancient Mesopotamia not considered "Sacred Scripture"? What comprises "Sacred Scripture"?

BIBLIOGRAPHY

Collins, Paul. "An Overview of Ancient Mesopotamian History." Accessed March 12, 2012. http://www.gatewaystobabylon.com/myths/whymeso .htm.

Dalley, Stephanie. *Myths from Mesopotamia: Gilgamesh, the Flood, and Others*. Oxford: Oxford University Press, 1991.

Foster, Benjamin R. *From Distant Days: Myths, Tales, and Poetry of Ancient Mesopotamia*. Bethesda, MD: CDL Press, 1995.

Hallo, William W., ed. *Canonical Compositions from the Biblical World*. Vol. 1 of *The Context of Scripture*. Leiden: Brill, 1997.

Matthews, Victor H., and Don C. Benjamin. *Old Testament Parallels: Laws and Stories from the Ancient Near East*. New York / Mahwah, NJ: Paulist Press, 1991.

Pritchard, James B., ed. *Ancient Near Eastern Texts Relating to the Old Testament*. 3rd ed. Princeton: Princeton University Press, 1969.

Chapter 4

WHAT IS CULTURE CRITICISM OF THE OLD TESTAMENT?

Gale A. Yee

READ GENESIS 3 AND EXODUS 1–15

The Bible is often called the "Living Word of God." The Bible "lives" in the homilies we hear during our eucharistic celebrations, in the learned interpretations of our biblical scholars and theologians, and even in our devotional reading of the text. But the Bible also "lives" in the many cultural manifestations of the Bible in art, literature, poetry, music, and film. These wonderful displays of imagination and vision inspire our faith. We marvel at the depth and breadth of human creativity as it expresses its encounter with the biblical text. We are stirred during a rousing performance the Hallelujah Chorus of Handel's *Messiah*, which drew much of its libretto from the prophet Isaiah. We become emotionally overwhelmed as we gaze up at the ceiling of the Sistine Chapel and behold Michelangelo's frescoes of the Book of Genesis. Our souls effervesce with joy upon hearing Gerard Manley Hopkins's poetic meditation on God's creation, "Pied Beauty." Each of these cultural manifestations of the Bible retells the ancient stories anew, often in provocative ways that challenge our faith, as well as inspire it. This chapter will explore how visual culture shapes the way we read the biblical text. It will first introduce the reader to the emerging field of cultural criticism, as it is applied to the study of the Bible. It will then look at the ways in which the biblical stories have been translated into visual media such as painting and film.

Society often esteems as "cultured" those with highborn or upper-class tastes in the arts or the humanities. Culture however is much more. All people inhabit cultures of some sort. Culture is a language, set of codes, or symbols through which people share ideas, beliefs, and values in common. Culture reinforces the various ways in which people interrelate socially. Its codes are often embodied in spoken or written texts, in material artifacts, in art and song, in certain ways of behaving during times of peace and times of conflict. Culture provides identities for people that connect and bind them together. We can speak of ancient cultures like the Mayan or Celtic, or various ethnic cultures of the modern world, or particular segments of these, such as youth, immigrant, or gay subcultures. The Bible "lives" in various ways in and through these dramatically diverse cultures.

Because culture is exemplified in so many aspects of a functioning society, cultural criticism (or cultural studies) encompasses a range of academic disciplines, such as anthropology, history, literature, music, art history, sociology, and economics. The first phase of cultural studies as a discipline focused on retrieving cultures that were marginalized or overlooked in these disciplines, such as the working classes, the peasantry, and poor or destitute. Instead of concentrating on the "high" culture of the elite, cultural criticism attended to the various manifestations of "popular" culture, displayed among the common people. It studied the practices and objects of everyday life, and the uses and meanings which people gave them, such as comic books, pulp novels, or children's literature. The emergence of gender, race, and sexuality as important categories of analysis mobilized cultural studies to incorporate the insights of feminist theory, critical racial-ethnic theory, and queer theory in its second phase of development. Here one can analyze cultural phenomena such as romance novels, hip-hop music, or drag queen balls. Through advances in technology and the onset of global capitalism, cultural criticism enters a third phase, engaging postcolonial theory to analyze the power relations among cultures encountering each other internationally in cooperation and/or conflict. For example, some women in Middle Eastern countries continue to wear the veil, usually considered a symbol of female submission, as an act of resistance against Western cultural imperialism.

THE BIBLE IN HIGH AND POPULAR CULTURE

A cultural critic can examine the place and role of the Bible in high and popular Western culture through the ages and in a myriad of places globally. For much of history, only a small portion of the population was literate. Many common folk therefore learned the narratives of the Bible visually through great works of art in churches and cathedrals, such as stained glass windows, carvings, mosaics, and paintings. A common block-book of pictures called the *Biblia Pauperum* ("Paupers' Bible") also circulated as teaching aids for clergy for those who could not read. Possessing the written Bible as a material object initially belonged to certain groups, such as the religious orders in medieval monasteries that painstakingly transcribed and richly illustrated the book, and the wealthy who were able to afford one. Prior to the sixteenth century, the Bible as a book was primarily an artifact of high culture. However, with the invention of the printing press that reproduced the Bible cheaply, the translation of the Bible from the original Hebrew and Greek into the vernacular, and Christian missionary activity to non-Western lands, the Bible entered the realm of popular culture. Theoretically, anyone was able to own a Bible in his or her household. The ubiquitous Gideon Bible could be found not only in hotel rooms, but also in hospitals, convalescent homes, medical offices, domestic violence shelters, prisons, and jails.

Let's focus on the Bible in contemporary U.S. consumer culture. As the best-selling book of all time, the Bible is a hot commercial commodity. Although revered as a sacred book, it is also a source of big business enterprises that are eager to supply Bibles for the different demands of the marketplace and benefit economically off them. Visiting a Christian bookstore, one is inundated by the many translations of the Bible, as well as the variety of colors, sizes, and prices to fit any taste or budget. There are big heavy family Bibles, which record the births, marriages, and deaths of family members, and small ones that slip easily into shirt pockets. There are the shelves of devotional Bibles for brides, for married couples, for singles, for men seeking biblical models of masculinity and maturity, for women in recovery, for soldiers, for grandmothers, for sportsmen, and so forth. Although many of the illustrated Bibles are geared toward children or teens, the American artist R. Crumb created a graphic version, *The Book of Genesis* (2009), containing adult themes. *The People's Bible* (2009) interprets the biblical texts from diverse racial, ethnic, and multicultural contexts. For the ecologically minded, *The Green Bible* (2008) highlights in green the passages that speak to God's care for creation, and is made from recycled paper and printed with soy-based ink. Bibles featuring Jewish scholars are *The Jewish Study Bible* (2004), commenting on the Tanak (the Hebrew Scriptures), and *The Jewish Annotated New Testament* (2011), which underscores the Jewish contexts in which the New Testament was produced. Many of these Bibles come in large-print editions, compact editions, and as e-books and audio books on cassettes, CDs, and in MP3 format. Besides the Bibles themselves, there is the array of Bible accessories, such as Bible book covers (leather and plastic), book tabs, dry highlighters, bookmarks, maps, and timelines that one can purchase. Also in the marketplace is a whole line of Bible action figures for Noah, Moses, David and Goliath, and Samson. The Daniel action figure is supplied with his own lion and lioness. A cultural critic would investigate the ways in which the Bible functions for different social groups at the popular level and who actually profits financially from its sale.

Even more astounding than the huge financial income from the sale of Bibles is the fact that even though many Americans own a Bible, they generally do not read it. According to a 2007 *Time* cover story, only one-half of U.S. adults could name one of the four Gospels. Most could not name the first book of the Bible, Genesis. The comedian Jay Leno once asked his audience to name one of the Ten Commandments. One ventured: "'God helps those who help themselves?'" No one could name any of the apostles, but most knew the names of the Beatles. Some surveys discovered that 12 percent of adults believe that Joan of Arc was Noah's wife and that 50 percent of high school seniors thought Sodom and Gomorrah were husband and wife. A cultural critic would examine this wide gulf between the possession of Bibles and the biblical illiteracy in the population. Certain questions would govern her investigation: What circumstances and hidden cultural assumptions govern the use of the Bible in a particular place and time? How do different parts of the population invest meaning in the Bible and how may this cohere or conflict with the meaning the Bible had for other groups? How do the particular cultures that people inhabit, such as women's groups, youth groups, LGBT groups, and so on, interface with their interpretation of the Bible? Such studies will undoubtedly reveal that the meanings of the biblical text, like those of other cultural products, depend on who is using them, at what time, in what place, and for what reason.

THE BIBLE AND VISUAL CULTURE

The Bible's well-known and beloved stories have inspired painters, sculptors, architects, and other visual artists for centuries. These works display the various ways in which these artists interpreted the biblical text. Original works of art inspired by the Bible can be viewed directly in churches, museums, and art galleries. Several "coffee table" books assemble many artistic masterpieces in vivid color, one of these devoted exclusively to women in the Bible (see the bibliography). One need not go to a museum or buy a coffee table book to view these paintings, however. If one has access to the Internet, there are many sites devoted to the Bible in art, such as http://www.biblical-art.com/index.htm, http://www.artbible.info/ and http://catholic-resources.org/Art/. Many collections of important museums can also be found on the Web (http://www.artcom.com/Museums/index.htm), which can be searched to find other examples of biblical art.

Visual artists have invested their works not only with the aesthetic, moral, and theological values of their culture and times but also have imprinted upon them their notions of gender, race, class, and sexuality. Because most Americans have never actually read the Bible, nor are they conscious of its ancient Near Eastern cultural setting, their notions of the biblical stories are already imbued with the mental pictures they've garnered from popular culture. We will observe this not only in the discussion of biblical paintings and sculptures, but also in advertisements and films based on the Bible. We think of Michelangelo's gray-haired, old white male on the ceiling in the Sistine Chapel when reading about the creator God in Genesis. Michelangelo fashioned his statue of David according to Greek ideals of the body during the Renaissance, which probably did not resemble the historical King David at all. Jesus himself is often depicted as a white man with long blond hair and blue eyes. However, since Mel Gibson's *The Passion of the Christ*, Jim Caviezel's brunette Jesus can come to mind. Comparing the biblical text with its visual depiction can help us to develop both our reading and seeing skills. We become aware that the biblical text can have multiple interpretations, not just one, when we actually see these interpretations in different works of art. We learn what actually is or is not in the biblical text, and what are later expansions of it. At the same time, we will discover how other cultures have encountered and retold it visually.

Let us take, for example, depictions of the Adam and Eve story. Genesis 3 is often referred to as the "temptation story," with Eve "tempting" Adam to sin. Christian history is replete with statements by theologians and writers blaming the "fall of man" on woman, justifying her subordination by appealing to Genesis 3:

- "From a woman sin had its beginning, and because of her we all die." (Sir 25:24)
- Tertullian on women: "Do you not know that you are Eve. The sentence of God on this sex of yours lives in this age: the guilt of necessity must live too. *You* are the Devil's gateway. *You* are the unsealer of that forbidden tree. *You* are the first deserter of the divine Law. *You* are she who persuaded him whom the Devil was not valiant enough to attack. *You* destroyed so easily God's image man. On account of *your* desert, that is death, even the Son of God had to die." (Tertullian, *Cult. fem.*, 1, 1) [Writing during the second and third centuries, Tertullian has been called the "Father of Latin Christianity."]
- "For though the devil tempted Eve to sin, yet Eve seduced Adam. And as the sin of Eve would not have brought death to our soul and body unless the sin had afterwards passed on to Adam, to which he was tempted by Eve, not by the devil, therefore she is more bitter than death." (*Malleus Maleficarum* 1, 6) [A manual written in the 1400s by two Dominican inquisitors in witchcraft investigations.]
- "What kind of a part does Eve play? If we can believe the story, she is the seducer. Without her that primal sin would never have been committed. Everything for Eve! Adam's fault was that he yielded to her. It seems that there is nothing left

> to his descendants but to regret his complacency." (Theodore
> Reik, *Myth and Guilt*, 110) [a prominent psychoanalyst, one of
> Freud's first students in Vienna]

Taking their cues from the sexist views of their time, cultural representations of Eve, both ancient and modern, often feature a voluptuous white woman with long blond hair and blue eyes. She is frequently positioned seductively, holding out an apple to Adam. A phallic snake slithers somewhere in the background or even sensuously around the woman's body. For some examples, see

- Hendrik Goltzius's "Fall of Man" online http://www.nga.gov/content/ngaweb/Collection/art-object-page.95659.html
- the explicit ad for Cisco systems, http://www.spike.com/video-clips/hab8ye/strange-adam-and-eve-inspired-ad-for-cisco;
- and the gay version of the Centraal Beheer commercial, http://www.youtube.com/watch?v=zKAW96N-Vms.

Let us go back to the original text and read what is actually there. First of all, there is no physical description of Eve. Although the original author most likely imagined an ancient Semitic female, Western visualizers have rendered Eve according to the idealized conceptions of the female body of their time. Given the cultural dominance of Euro-American illustrators of the Bible, Eve was usually portrayed as a white female.

Second, there is no description of the fruit as an apple, red or green. The Hebrew word *pĕrî* simply means "fruit" and can cover a variety of species such as olives, grapes, figs, apricots, citrons, and pomegranates, among others. About the tree of the knowledge of good and evil which produced the fruit, we do know that

- God commanded the man not to eat of this tree, for on the day that he ate from it, he would die (Gen 2:16);
- the woman saw that the tree was good for food;
- it was a delight to the eyes;
- it was to be desired to make one wise (Gen 3:6a).

Third, there is no sexual seduction scene. Because of the attributes of the tree (good for food; pleasing to look at; a source of wisdom), the woman "took of its fruit and ate; and she also gave some to her husband, who was with her, and he ate" (Gen 3:6b). The woman was simply offering her man good food, not only food that was delightful in appearance, but also one that could make them wise. Wisdom is a superior quality that we all strive to possess. In giving the fruit to the man, the woman was motivated positively, with no inherently sexual or evil intent.

Fourth, the man was with the woman during the interchange with the snake. He, not the woman, was the one to whom God originally commanded not to eat of the tree. He should have been the one to resist the snake. Yet, the text says that "he ate."

Many of us unconsciously come to the biblical text with cultural "baggage" that influences our reading of Scripture. As we have just seen in the famous story of Adam and Eve, it is therefore important to become aware of the secondary interpretations of culture, bracket these for the time being, and read the biblical text closely with fresh eyes. We will then be better positioned to understand the biblical text on its own terms, and how culture reinterprets and expands upon it. Especially in the visual representation of the first woman in Genesis, we also become aware of how culture can sometimes distort the biblical text to fit prevailing views of gender, race, and sexuality.

THE BIBLE ON HOLLYWOOD AND VINE

Besides the Adam and Eve story, another biblical tale that has been vividly imprinted upon the North American cultural consciousness is the story of Moses and the Exodus. Even though most people in congregations have not actually read the Exodus story in its entirety, they may have seen the big-screen versions *The Ten Commandments* (1956), directed by Cecil B. DeMille, and the animated rendering *The Prince of Egypt* (1998). Even though Moses is not physically described in the Bible, it is hard to visualize Moses in the U.S. context without thinking first of Charlton Heston, former president of the NRA. In a publicity photo op, Heston's profile was set side by side with Michelangelo's famous statue of Moses, to reveal their uncanny similarity.

Comparing the biblical text with these two films offers an excellent opportunity for congregations to learn about the biblical text, share a communal experience of watching two fine movies, and engage in some aspects of cultural criticism. Congregations should begin with a close reading of Exodus 1–20, and 32 (the golden calf episode), which are selectively depicted in *The Ten Commandments*. *The Prince of Egypt* basically stops at Exodus 15, providing only a brief glimpse of the giving of the law on Sinai (Exodus 19–20). Even in this close reading, participants should be aware that the chapters omitted from the films are major pieces of the biblical story itself. God freed the Israelites from Egyptian slavery, not as an end in itself, but to enter into a covenantal relationship with the deity in the wilderness. God's continual command to the Pharaoh through Moses was, "Let my people go, so that they may worship me in the wilderness" (5:1; 7:16; 8:1, 20; 9:1, 13; 10:3. Cf. 6:6–7). The crucial notion of covenant between God and Israel and Israel's covenantal observances have been omitted in both films.

Because there is so much packed into Exodus 1–20, 32, it would be best to discuss it in sections:

- Exodus 1–6: the enslavement, birth of Moses, his commissioning at the burning bush;
- Exodus 7–15: the plague stories; Passover; deliverance at the Red Sea;
- Exodus 16–20, 32: the wilderness stories; the giving of the law; the golden calf.

Since the film versions are admixtures of visual and aural forms, participants should read the biblical stories out loud to each other, jotting down any images that come to mind from the hearing. These images may have been triggered by previous cultural encounters with the story, perhaps prior viewings of the films themselves. For each section, participants should discuss some of the following:

- Who are the main characters involved in the story? Make sure you include God as one of these characters.
- What do we know about these characters? Take special note of the gender, race, and class of the characters.
- What do they do, or how do they function in the story?
- What did you previously know about the Exodus story and what have you now learned through this close reading?
- Have any previous conceptions of the Exodus story come from cultural reinterpretations of it? If so, which ones? Did they enhance, transform, or alter the biblical story?

After the close reading sessions, the participants can now compare the biblical story to their filmic versions. *The Ten Commandments* and *The Prince of Egypt* should be viewed on separate occasions, following a similar process in analyzing the movies.

- Note the main characters in the film, including God, and what they do. Take note of the gender, race, and class of the characters in the film.
- How are their portrayals the same as or different from the biblical story?
- Which biblical characters are omitted from the film version? Does this make a difference?
- What characters in the film are added to the biblical story? Are these characters involved in subplots that diverge from the

main narrative? Do these characters and plots enhance the original story or detract from it?

- Is the film faithful to the biblical story or does it alter or distort it? How?
- How does the film reflect the time in which it was produced (the 1950s for *The Ten Commandments*, and the late 1990s for *The Prince of Egypt*)?
- Note that *The Ten Commandments* is a film played by human actors, while *The Prince of Egypt* is an animation of the story with animated characters. How does the medium (film, animation) affect the understanding of the Exodus story?
- How do music and song add or detract in *The Prince of Egypt* from the story of the Exodus?
- What are your overall reactions to the film and animation, compared with the biblical text?

Both filmic versions transform the Exodus story in their own particular ways. Both emphasize the Exodus story in epic proportions. In particular, *The Ten Commandments* added and developed a number of characters and plots that were either not in the biblical text or played minor roles in it. Although God appears in both renditions, "he" has no visible form and becomes more of an agent to advance the plot than a developed character. Rather than a story of God saving the Hebrews, both films highlight instead the rivalry between Moses and the Pharaoh Rameses. In *The Ten Commandments* this rivalry was thoroughly antagonistic, especially fueled by their competition over the same woman, Nefretiri. In *The Prince of Egypt*, the relationship between the two in the beginning was affectionate and brotherly, until Moses becomes the leader of the Israelite slaves. Moreover, in contrast to his portrayal in *The Ten Commandments*, Rameses in *The Prince of Egypt* was more likeable and engaging, and his defeat at the end evokes sympathy and compassion from the viewer.

Both films were products of their times. *The Ten Commandments* was produced during the 1950s' anti-Communist McCarthy era. At the beginning of the film, DeMille asserts: "The theme of this picture is whether men are to be ruled by God's law or whether they are to be ruled by the whims of a dictator like Rameses. Are men the property of the state? Or are they free souls under God? This same battle continues throughout the world today."

Anti-Soviet themes are suggested in the juxtaposition of the Russian-born actor Yul Brynner playing hardhearted Rameses with the all-American Charlton Heston embodying the savior Moses. Critics have noted that Moses' pose at the end of the movie evokes the Statue of Liberty. Although battles over African American racial discrimination and segregation were fought during the 1950s, these ironically were not taken up in *The Ten Commandments*,

an archetypal story about the emancipation of exploited slaves. Aside from
the exotic otherness of Yul Brynner, the main characters of *The Ten
Commandments* were played by white actors.

Seeking to communicate with a global audience, the 1990s' *The Prince
of Egypt*, on the other hand, darkened the skin tones of all of its animated
characters and depicted them with more "ethnic-looking" features. The pro-
ducers of *The Prince of Egypt* wanted a film that would appeal to and not
offend the widest possible religious audience. The Exodus story was thus
reduced to the lowest common denominator. This was epitomized in the
lyrics of its Oscar-winning song, "When You Believe," sung by pop stars
Mariah Carey and Whitney Houston:

> There can be miracles
> When you believe—
> Though hope if frail,
> It's hard to kill.
> Who knows what miracles
> You can achieve
> When you believe
> Somehow you will—
> Now you will,
> You will when you believe.

Although the music itself was very inspiring, these bland lyrics would
be appropriate for any Jewish, Christian, Muslim or even secular audience on
different points of the theological continuum.

Both films departed from the biblical text particularly from the perspective of gender. The story of the midwives (Exod 1:15–21) was omitted from
both movies to their detriment. As a subversive tale of resistance, this biblical
story pits lower-class women against the highest ruler of the land. The security
of Pharaoh's great empire paradoxically rests on these two seemingly powerless
women. Note that in the biblical text the midwives are named, while the
Pharaoh is not, highlighting their importance for the overall narrative.

The Moses-Nefretiri-Rameses triangle was the biggest innovation of
The Ten Commandments. The addition of a fully developed female character
to the predominantly male biblical story, however, did not strike a chord for
women's rights. Nefretiri is the pampered, lustful daughter of the Pharaoh
who murdered her maid Memnet to prevent Memnet from revealing the
Hebrew ethnic origin of her lover, Moses. Nefretiri represents the seductive
allure of Egypt, as she continually tries to induce Moses to forsake the
Hebrews and return to her. Though theologically problematic, the biblical
text is clear that God hardens Pharaoh's heart in the story (4:21; 7:3; 14:4, 17).
In the movie, however, Nefretiri becomes the manipulative agent through

whom Rameses' heart was "hardened," telling Moses, "Who else can soften Pharaoh's heart or harden it?" Moses responds, "Yes, you may be the lovely dust for which God will work his purpose." Nefretiri, the woman scorned, goads Rameses into refusing Moses' request to free the slaves. When, after the death of his firstborn son, Rameses allows the slaves to go, Nefretiri ridicules him until he pursues them to his utter defeat. The movie thus places the origin of the plagues and especially the death of the firstborn of Egypt on the female character, not on God.

Women fare better in *The Prince of Egypt*. Moses meets his feisty future wife, Tzipporah, at a court gathering, when she is offered to him by Rameses as a sexual prisoner. When Moses enters his bedroom to claim his prize, he discovers that Tzipporah had disarmed her guards and escaped. Unlike the biblical story, it is Tzipporah, not Moses' brother Aaron, who accompanies Moses to Egypt to confront Pharaoh in his court (cf. 7:1–2). Expanding the biblical text, Moses' sister Miriam is the one who informs Moses of his true identity in the film. She sings the song of his birth that sets the stage for the dream sequence where he remembers his mother and sister fleeing the massacre of the Hebrew boys. At Miriam's cry for help at the abuse of a slave, Moses responds. The biblical text simply has Moses seeing an Egyptian beating a slave and killing him (2:11–12). *The Prince of Egypt* is thus more woman-friendly than *The Ten Commandments*, most likely because of gains in women's rights since the 1950s.

Watching these two feature films on the Exodus as a group would be an excellent way for your congregations to experience cultural studies in action. When they read and study the text firsthand, they will come to know the wondrous power of this beloved story of liberation. They may learn aspects of the narrative that they have never read or heard before. They will also see how Hollywood transforms it: into an unrequited love story in *The Ten Commandments*, on the one hand, and a tale of ruptured brotherly relations in *The Prince of Egypt*, on the other. Viewing these films can also be a "fun-filled," inexpensive, bonding event, a congregation's "night out" to see two very well-done movies on one of the most significant events of Israel's salvation history. And it may be a very moving and spiritual experience for the group.

CONCLUSION

Cultural criticism is one of the newer methods of interpreting the biblical texts. It analyzes the different ways in which the Bible has been received and interpreted in the different cultures that encounter it. Cultural criticism can analyze the reinterpretations of Scripture within both high culture and popular culture. It can investigate Scripture's reception history in its various iterations from very early times all the way up to the present.

In this chapter, we saw first how the Bible is an important economic cultural commodity in the U.S. context. Next, we analyzed the translation of the Bible into several different forms of visual media: painting, commercials, motion pictures, and animated films. We observed how we already have mental images of the biblical stories, because of our prior encounter with them in these different cultural manifestations in which the biblical stories appear. In exploring these forms, we need to develop both our reading and seeing skills, to see exactly what is written in the text and the many different ways in which culture modifies, transforms, alters, or distorts it. Because these different renderings of the Bible are products of their times, we must pay particular attention to how gender, race, class, and other factors play into the depiction of the story. Cultural criticism offers one way to evaluate the many different and exciting ways in which the various cultures we inhabit encounter, appropriate, and venerate this sacred text.

QUESTIONS

1. Where do the Bible stories, characters, sayings, and so forth appear in your everyday life? For example, in cartoons, advertisements, a pet store named Noah's Ark, a rock band named Jonah and the Whales.

2. Do you have a Bible in your home? What kind of Bible is it? Is it a family heirloom? Which English translation? Where is it located? Do you read it? If not, what is it used for?

3. Examine the artwork in your church. Are there any depictions of the Bible found there? Compare this artwork with the biblical text. What part of the story is highlighted in the artwork? What part of the story is missing? Does the artwork make you appreciate the Bible story better or not? Why?

4. Share poems, music, literature, and paintings based on the Bible with your study group and lead a discussion on them.

BIBLIOGRAPHY

Babington, Bruce, and Peter William Evans. *Biblical Epics: Sacred Narrative in the Hollywood Cinema*. Manchester: Manchester University Press, 1993.

Bernard, Bruce. *The Bible and Its Painters*. New York: Macmillan, 1983.

Calderhead, Christopher, ed. *The Bible Portrayed in 200 Masterpieces of Painting*. Old Saybrook, CT: Konecky & Konecky, 2005.

Frankel, Ellen, ed. *The Illustrated Hebrew Bible: 75 Selected Stories*. New York: Abradale Press, 1999.

Gunn, David M. "Cultural Criticism: Viewing the Sacrifice of Jephthah's Daughter." In *Judges and Method: New Approaches in Biblical Studies*, edited by Gale A. Yee, 202–36. 2nd ed. Minneapolis: Fortress Press, 2007.

Henry, Avril, ed. *Biblia Pauperum: A Facsimile and Edition*. Ithaca, NY: Cornell University Press, 1987.

Langston, Scott M. *Exodus Through The Centuries*. Blackwell Bible Commentaries. Malden, MA: Blackwell, 2006.

Sawyer, John F. A. *The Blackwell Companion to the Bible and Culture*. Malden, MA: Blackwell, 2006.

Sölle, Dorothée, Joe H. Kirchberger, and Anne-Marie Schnieper-Müller. *Great Women of the Bible in Art and Literature*. Grand Rapids, MI: Eerdmans, 1993.

Wright, Melanie Jane. "Coming in From the Cold (War): Cecil B. DeMille's *The Ten Commandments* (1956)." In *Moses in America: The Cultural Uses of Biblical Narrative*, 89–127. New York: Oxford University Press, 2002.

Chapter 5

WHY DOES GOD HAVE MANY NAMES IN THE OLD TESTAMENT AND WHY DO WE NEED THEM?

John L. McLaughlin

READ GENESIS 1–3, 6–9, AND THE TEXTS DISCUSSED BELOW

The Old Testament uses many words and phrases to refer to God, which some may find confusing. Surely it would be simpler if there was a single way of referring to God. But even though the biblical texts went through many stages before reaching their current form, the various editors left the different terms in the texts, because they saw value in this divergence. By examining the different ways to identify God we gain insight into the diverse ways in which the ancient Israelites understood what God does and how God relates to humans. The various terms for God also point to more than one religious tradition within the Old Testament, resulting in a richer understanding of the Bible. This is best seen in the Pentateuch, the first five books of the Bible, where different words for God indicate separate theological traditions, which in turn helps explain duplications and even contradictions within the biblical text.

YAHWEH

The most frequent term used for Israel's God is "Yahweh," which appears more than 6,600 times in the Hebrew text (actually, the earliest texts

57

only wrote the consonants, namely YHWH). However, over time YHWH was increasingly understood as sacred and therefore not pronounced. Instead, when devout Jews saw those four consonants, they said something else, such as "God," "The Name" or *adonay*, which is Hebrew for "My Lord." When rabbis inserted lines, dots, and dashes above and below the Hebrew consonants about a thousand years ago to represent the vowels, they inserted the vowels for *adonay*, the word they most often spoke. These vowels combined with JHVH (the equivalent of YHWH in medieval Latin) produce "Jehovah," which was then mistakenly taken as the name of God. This is comparable to inserting the vowel from "cat" into the consonants from "dog"; the result is "dag," which is no more an English word than "Jehovah" is a real Hebrew word. Instead, most modern English translations render the word as "LORD." Using all capital letters indicates that this represents "Yahweh," whereas "lord" in lower case letters translates the Hebrew word for one's superior.

Yahweh is a combination of the letter *Y*, representing the pronoun "he/it" and *HWH*, the Hebrew verb "to be." Most scholars agree that the verb is in the causative form, and since the Israelites thought of God as a person, the word meant "he causes to be." They also considered all deities to be either male or female, and Yahweh was identified as male. The references to Israel's God as "he" in this essay reflects their understanding rather than any claim as to God's true nature.

The formulation "he causes to be" indicates that the Israelites understood Yahweh as the creator. As a result, we frequently find the phrase "LORD of hosts," and the presence of all capital letters in LORD indicates that this is "Yahweh." Therefore, the phrase means "he creates the hosts" (or "armies," the root meaning of the Hebrew word). The hosts were the stars, which the ancients understood to be divine beings who made up the heavenly army. Thus, Yahweh is linked to the creation of both the physical and the divine realms and their inhabitants. Yahweh was also understood to have created Israel as a nation through the Exodus. Yahweh did not just liberate some slaves from Egypt, he led them to Mt. Sinai in order to establish a covenant with them. At Sinai God gave them laws that regulated their relationships with both God and one another. Therefore, Exodus was a central feature of Israelite religion, alongside the insistence on Yahweh's centrality in their lives. Because Yahweh alone liberated them from Egypt, no other gods could replace him, because that would mean losing the connection to what he had done for them in the Exodus event. They would cease to be the people Yahweh had saved from slavery.

ELOHIM

The second most common way to refer to Israel's God was the word "Elohim." This is the plural of the Hebrew word for "god," and is used for groups of non-Israelite deities such as the gods of Egypt (Exod 12:2), of Syria, Sidon, Moab, the Ammonites, and the Philistines (Judg 10:6), of the Amorites (Josh 24:15; Judg 6:10), and so on. But "Elohim" is often used with singular verbs, indicating a single god, and the context usually indicates that this is Israel's God, that is, Yahweh. In fact, Elohim often serves as an alternative name for Yahweh. For instance, the wording of Psalms 14 and 53 is virtually identical, except that the first one uses Yahweh and the second one uses Elohim. Similarly, the Book of Chronicles copies large sections from Samuel and Kings but regularly changes Yahweh to Elohim.

Using a plural noun to refer to Israel's god is usually explained in one of two ways. The first is that it is a "plural of majesty" similar to the royal "we" used today by kings, queens, and popes. However, the royal "we" was not an ancient practice, and God never uses the plural "we" as a self reference in the Old Testament (God's use of "us" in Gen 1:26; 3:22 is best understood as an address to other heavenly beings). Moreover, even in modern usage, people only use the pronoun "we" but never a noun in the plural. For instance, while Benedict XVI may have referred to himself as "we," he never referred to himself as "the popes," nor does anyone else. A more theological interpretation of using the plural form "Elohim" for Israel's God is that the roles and attributes given to a foreign nation's many gods are found within Israel's one God. But single foreign gods are also referred to as "Elohim" within the Bible: Astarte, Chemosh, and Milcom are each called the Elohim of the Sidonians, Moab, and Ammon respectively (1 Kgs 11:33), while Baal-zebub is called the "Elohim of Ekron," a Philistine city (2 Kgs 1:2, 3, 6, 16). In light of these texts, a better explanation of using the plural Elohim for a single deity is as a plural of intensification, indicating the most important god of a particular group. Just as Astarte, Chemosh, Milcom, and Baal-zebub are each the chief god in their respective lands, so too Yahweh is the most important God for the Israelites.

YAHWEH AND ELOHIM IN THE PENTATEUCH

The use of both Yahweh and Elohim in the Pentateuch has led to the identification of different streams of tradition within the first five books of the Bible. This is not just a matter of different terms being used for Israel's deity, which could be explained as stylistic variation to avoid repeating the same term over and over. Rather, there are clusters of terms linked to these two words. For instance, when the word Yahweh appears, the Ten Commandments are given at Mt. Sinai, the father of the twelve tribes is named Israel, those already living in the land are Canaanites, and Moses' father-in-law is called either Reuel or Hobab. In contrast, when Elohim is used, we find Mt. Horeb, Jacob, Amorites, and Jethro. Moreover, the Hebrew used in these two clusters of terms reflects different stages in the development of the ancient language, just as modern readers can distinguish the English written by Chaucer and Shakespeare. As a result, scholars initially identified two sources within the Pentateuch, which they called the Yahwist and the Elohist, depending on the preferred term for Israel's God. For ease of reference, they were assigned letters based on those terms, namely J for the Yahwist (Jahwist in German) and E for the Elohist.

Recognizing these two sources helps explain duplications in the Pentateuch. For instance, in Genesis 6:19–20 God (Elohim) tells Noah to bring two of every animal into the ark, and verse 22 says, "Noah did this; he did all that God commanded him." Then, in Genesis 7:1–3 Yahweh (or "the LORD" in most English translations) tells him to take seven pairs of clean animals and one pair of unclean animals, and once again, "Noah did all that the LORD had commanded him" (v. 5). Another example of duplication starts in Genesis 12:10–20, where Abraham tells Pharaoh that Sarah is his wife, but Yahweh sends plagues to stop Pharaoh from sleeping with her. Then, in Genesis 20:1–18 Abraham says the same thing to Abimelech, a Canaanite king, but God (Elohim) warns him in a dream not to sleep with Sarah. There is even a third version of this story in Genesis 26:6–11, where Isaac tells the same Abimelech that Rebekah is his wife, but Abimelech sees them being intimate and realizes they are husband and wife.

It is possible to reconcile these repeated stories, although some difficulties will still remain. For instance, Noah could have received two different commands as to how many animals to take and of which kind, but why did the deity, whatever word is used, not just give Noah the larger figure the first time? There is also a mathematical problem: since Noah had already brought one pair of every kind of animal onto the ark, if he followed the second command literally, as Genesis 7:5 suggests, there would actually be two pairs of unclean animals and eight pairs of clean animals. Granted, Noah may not have interpreted God's word literally, but the simplest solution is to attribute the duplications to two different sources.

It is also possible that the three stories of a patriarch and his wife came from a single author. Abraham could have played the same trick on different foreign rulers, especially since he profited handsomely from this ploy the first time (and did again the second time). However, each time he jeopardized God's promise of direct descendants (Gen 14:4), since Sarah could have been impregnated by either Pharaoh or Abimelech. But perhaps he did not interpret the plagues the first time as a divine warning not to do it again. Similarly, Abimelech may have been so abysmally stupid as to fall for the same deception by a father and his son. But these problems are removed if we recognize the first and third stories as coming from the Yahwist and the second one deriving from the Elohist. In that case, within each narrative stream Abraham only jeopardizes the line of descent once and Abimelech is only duped once, although by different individuals. Only when the two larger narratives are combined do difficulties arise.

Nevertheless, ancient peoples may not have shared our modern views of logic and consistency, and a single author could have written such duplications. However, some texts directly contradict each other, such as the creation stories in Genesis 1 and 2. In Genesis 1 God (Elohim) speaks over the course of six days and creates the sky, oceans, land, and all the things that live and grow in or on them, including humans, whereas in Genesis 2 the LORD (Yahweh) makes a human being out of the ground. A common explanation of this apparent repetition is that the first story deals with creation on a large scale, describing the origins of the world and its inhabitants as a whole, while Genesis 2 focuses on the creation of humankind. An even more ingenious reconciliation of the two stories is that in Genesis 1 God created the cavemen and cavewomen, but they were not good enough so God created true human beings in Genesis 2. This had the added benefit of explaining where Cain got his wife (Gen 4:17): he married a cavewoman. But the beings in Genesis 1:26–27 were made "in the image and likeness of God" and if they were "not good enough" that means God's image and likeness are flawed. Moreover, in Genesis 1 those supposed cavemen were made *after all* the plants and animals but in Genesis 2 the "human beings" were made *before any* plants or animals existed. The order of creation in the two stories is contradictory and cannot be reconciled. Another set of texts is equally problematic. Genesis 4:26 states that humans began to call upon the name of Yahweh during the time of Enosh, Adam's grandson, while Exodus 3:13–16 and 6:3 both assert that the name Yahweh was revealed for the first time to Moses just before the Exodus. These contradictory claims cannot be explained if they were written by a single author. Instead, they indicate that we are dealing with more than one source within the Pentateuch.

In fact, scholars eventually identified more than just two sources within the Pentateuch. First, they noticed that Exodus 3:13–16 says that earlier generations knew Yahweh as "the God of your Fathers" while in Genesis 6:3 they knew him as "God Almighty." This difference led people to notice that some texts using Elohim also show a concern for matters of ritual, sacrifice, order, and so on. A prime example of this is Genesis 1. The passage is balanced into the first three days of creation, when God establishes light and darkness, sea and sky, and then dry land, after which God creates the things that exist in each area, namely the sun, moon, and stars (day four); fish and birds (day five); and plants, animals, and humans (day six). Then God rests on the seventh day, providing the basis for the Sabbath. Since things like ritual, sacrifice, the Sabbath, and so on, are primarily concerns of priests, this material, along with many of the cultic laws in the other books of the Pentateuch, was called the Priestly source, and assigned the letter P. Scholars also noticed distinctive vocabulary running through Deuteronomy, especially the repeated references to the deity as "the LORD your God" ("Yahweh, your Elohim"). This matches the book's insistence that the Israelites should worship only Yahweh because only he is their God, and should demonstrate their devotion by observing the laws found in the book. Thus, the Book of Deuteronomy was labeled D, or the Deuteronomistic source, within the Pentateuch.

Thus, scholars identified four streams of material in the Pentateuch, an idea named the Documentary Hypothesis. At first, people spoke of four written documents behind the Pentateuch, but today many are not convinced that all four existed in written form. For instance, E often reads like a supplement to J rather than a self-contained independent narrative. Similarly, P supplements the combined J and E, but also edits that material by inserting characteristically priestly concerns. Deuteronomy originally served as the introduction to the Books of Joshua, Judges, Samuel, and Kings and was only later linked to J, E, and P because of Moses' central role. Because of uncertainty whether or not these groups of material were written, I have used "tradition" or "stream," but "source" is acceptable as long as one does not insist that it means a written document.

Attention to different terms for the deity in the Pentateuch has value beyond reconciling duplicate stories. The four sources contain different perspectives on God's nature and how God interacts with humans. For instance, in J Yahweh is "anthropomorphic," acting like a human being. In Genesis 2 Yahweh "makes," "shapes," and "fashions" a human by molding clay with his hands and breathing into its nostrils. Yahweh also communicates directly with humans. In Genesis 3:8–19 he walks around the Garden of Eden and talks with the first humans about their transgression, then makes clothes for them (Gen 3:21). Similarly, in Genesis 17 Yahweh appears to Abraham to describe the covenant he will make with him, and they share a meal in Genesis 18:1–8.

In contrast, in the E material Elohim is more distant. Although God cares for humans as much as in the Yahwist, God does not speak with them directly. Instead Elohim communicates through dreams, as we saw above in the case of Abimelech in Genesis 20; or sends an angel, as when Hagar encounters "the angel of the LORD" in Genesis 16 and 21, when Moses sees the same figure in the burning bush (Exod 3:2), or when "the angel of the LORD" protects the Israelites from the Egyptians through the pillar of cloud (Exod 14:19). In the Priestly tradition God (Elohim) is even more distant, "creating" the world by speech alone in Genesis 1, versus the more engaging verbs in Genesis 2, and using the legal material in the Pentateuch to establish the cultic system, where contact with God is mediated through rituals managed by priests. Finally, Deuteronomy emphasizes the need for the Israelites to worship "Yahweh, your God" exclusively, with the positive or negative consequences of obedience and disobedience spelled out in detail.

By combining these different perspectives about God, rather than eliminating some of them, the editors of the Pentateuch affirmed that they were all valid. Rather than force their experiences of God into a single perspective, they acknowledged that God acted differently at different times and places. This means that God adapted divine revelation to different contexts, acting according to the needs of humans and their ability to understand God's action in their lives in diverse times and places.

EL: A NOUN AND A NAME

Another common term for God is "El," which is both the singular form of the Hebrew noun meaning "God" and the name of the chief Canaanite god. It is often clear from the context that "El" means "God," but there are places where "El" is best explained as a divine name, such as when "El" is followed by a noun expressing an attribute or characteristic. In Genesis 14:18–19 Melchizedek blesses Abraham by *el elyon*, in Genesis 16:13 Hagar names the deity she encountered *el roi*, and in Genesis 21:33 Abraham calls the LORD *el olam*. The NRSV renders these as "God Most high," "El-roi" (with a note that it means "God who sees"), and "the everlasting God" respectively. However, in ancient Hebrew this grammatical construction usually indicates a divine name, not the noun, plus an attribute, so they should be translated as "El, the Most High," "El who sees" and "El, the eternal one."

This is supported by evidence about the god El outside the Bible. First, "the eternal one" is consistent with El's depiction in non-Israelite texts as someone who is old, with white hair and a beard, as well as his title "the Father of Years." Second, since the phrase "the Most High" (*elyon*) is commonly used of superior individuals, both human and divine, it is an appropriate title for the chief god of a pantheon. Third, in Genesis 14:19 the Most High is called "maker of heaven and earth," echoing references to "El, creator of the earth" in two ancient inscriptions plus a mythological text. Therefore, it is not surprising to find Elyon alone in many biblical books, used either as a title or sometimes a name.

Another important combination of El and a title is "El Shaddai." This is commonly translated as "God Almighty," based on how the ancient Greek and Latin translations rendered it. But the second word probably means "the one of the mountains," which is consistent with El's dwelling place on the cosmic mountains and reflected in the phrase "the mountains of El/God" (Ps 36:6[E]). "El Shaddai" also appears in a non-Israelite mythological text and an inscription, while "Shaddai" appears alone both outside and inside the Bible. Shaddai as a title of El is supported by the former's appearance in a number of biblical poetic texts in parallel with El, and twice with Elyon. Moreover, thirty-one of the forty-one instances of Shaddai by itself are found in the Book of Job, which is set in the ancient past, demonstrating that it was understood as an ancient divine name. So too with the Priestly revelation of the name Yahweh to Moses in Exodus 6:3, which says that previously the Israelites knew Yahweh as El Shaddai.

This points to belief in a separate god named El, and that some in early Israel worshipped him instead of Yahweh. Two separate verses reinforce this view. In Genesis 33:20 Jacob dedicates an altar at Shechem to "El-Elohe-Israel." It is highly unlikely that both the singular ("El") and plural ("Elohe") forms of the noun "god" would be used in the same sentence one after another, especially when the singular noun can also be a divine name. It would make more sense to write "Elohim, the Elohe of Israel" in order to avoid any confusion as to the meaning. Therefore, the phrase in Genesis 33:20 should be translated as "El, the god of Israel." Similarly, in Genesis 46:3, God (Elohim) is revealed to Jacob as "God [el], the God [elohe] of your father," but once again the first word should be understood as the divine name rather than another form of the noun "god." Finally, note that Jacob's name is changed to Isra-el, not Isra-yah (using a short form of Yahweh).

Nevertheless, the Israelites quickly identified El and Yahweh as a single deity due to their many similarities. Both lived in a tent on a holy mountain seated upon cherubim, and were characterized as wise, benevolent, compassionate, and aged. As a result, the ancient Israelites blended these two deities into a single one at a very early stage in their religious development. They accepted the positive qualities of a non-Israelite deity that matched those of Yahweh, and once the two gods were combined all references to El in the Old Testament were easily understood to be about Yahweh. The result of this assimilation between Yahweh and El is seen in Daniel, one of the latest books of the Old Testament. Its date (ca. 169 BC) means that the book has a clearly monotheistic perspective, so any references to deities would have been understood as references to Yahweh. Thus, Yahweh is called "the Most High" in Daniel 3:26 and frequently in chapters 4, 5, and 7, while the description of the "Ancient One" (literally "Ancient of Days") in Daniel 7:9 parallels descriptions of El elsewhere, and the phrase itself recalls El's title, "the Father of Years." The idea of God as elderly and enduring is also reflected in Daniel 12:7 when a heavenly being swears by "the one who lives forever."

OTHER DIVINE NAMES AND TITLES

There are a number of less frequent names or titles for God in the Old Testament as well. One is "Eloah," a variation on the word El. Like El it sometimes means "god" and sometimes functions as a divine name, especially in Job, where it appears forty-one times (out of fifty-seven instances in the Bible), at times in parallel with Shaddai and El. Eloah is addressed directly in Psalm 139:19, indicating a divine name there as well. But apart from the Book of Job, which never mentions Yahweh in the poetic section, whether Eloah appears as a name or a noun, it is always understood to refer to Yahweh.

Another noun that sometimes serves as a name is "Lord" (*adon* in Hebrew). Used of both human and divine rulers, it indicates Yahweh's superiority over everyone and everything. The formula "my Lord" (*adonay*) refers exclusively to Yahweh, and was eventually spoken whenever the word Yahweh appeared in the Hebrew text (see above concerning "Jehovah"). When used independently of "Yahweh," "Lord" takes on characteristics of a divine name itself, such as when people pray directly to "Lord" (e.g., Gen 18:27; Exod 5:22; 34:9). Yahweh's rule over Israel is also conveyed by his frequent designation as King, so when the Israelites ask to have a king like the other nations they are rejecting Yahweh as their divine King (1 Sam 8:7; 10:19). A distinction between God and humans is also reflected in the title "the Holy One." Almost three-quarters of the time it is part of the longer phrase, "the Holy One of Israel," found mostly in Isaiah. In Psalm 71:22 the poet addresses "the Holy One of Israel" directly, indicating a divine name. Many times the phrase is found in connection with Israel's sinfulness, emphasizing the nation's contrast with Yahweh.

Three different titles are connected with each of the three patriarchs of Israel. In Genesis 31:42 Jacob says that "the God of my father, the Fear of Isaac" had blessed his actions while staying with his uncle and father-in-law, Laban, and in verse 53 Jacob swears by "the Fear of his father Isaac" when establishing a covenant with Laban. "The Fear of Isaac" indicates the dread God creates in others in order to protect Isaac and his son, Jacob, much like "the fear of Yahweh" in 1 Samuel 11:7; Isaiah 2:10; and so on. As such, the phrase describes God's activity and is not a name.

The phrase "the Mighty One of Jacob" occurs five times in the Old Testament, and "the Mighty One of Israel" is found once; all but one instance of the first phrase explicitly links it to Yahweh. Another possible translation is "the bull of Jacob," since the Hebrew consonants for "the mighty one" and "the bull" are identical, and there would have been no distinction in the Hebrew texts until vowels were added about a thousand years ago. "The bull of Jacob" is consistent with frequent connections between Yahweh and bulls in the Old Testament. A bull was also a common metaphor for strength and power, so either translation indicates God's might in relationship to humans, and especially God's protection of Jacob.

In Genesis 15:1 Yahweh tells Abraham, "I am your shield." A divine name comparable to those associated with the other two patriarchs may underlie this promise, namely "the Shield of Abraham." That very phrase occurs in the Hebrew text found after Sirach 51:12, in sequence with "the Rock of Isaac" (cf. "the Fear of Isaac" above) and "the Mighty One of Jacob." The title once again highlights Yahweh's protective presence for Abraham, and by extension his descendants.

In addition to the "Rock of Isaac" in Sirach 51:12, the term "rock" appears alone as both a title and a name for God. God as a metaphorical "rock" is reflected in the names Elizur ("My God is a Rock" [Num 1:5]) and Zurishaddai ("Shaddai is my rock" [Num 1:6]). "Rock" is a divine name in Pedahzur ("The Rock redeems" [Num 1:10]), as well as in Deuteronomy 32:4, 18, 30, and Habakkuk 1:12 addresses God directly as "O Rock." The word "rock" connotes God's strength, power, stability, and endurance. It is also synonymous with "mountain" and "crag," both of which convey a sense of refuge in numerous biblical texts, providing a metaphor for God's protection. "Rock" is often modified by adjectives highlighting specific aspects of God's activity toward the Israelites, such as "rock of...salvation," "...strength," and "...refuge," while Isaiah 26:4 describes Yahweh as "an everlasting rock," indicating God's unending protection.

Another term indicating God's protection was "warrior," as in Exodus 15:3—"The LORD is a warrior; the LORD is his name." This military role is also reflected in the title "The LORD of Hosts," which, we saw earlier, indicates God's creation of the heavenly armies. Sometimes this army intervened for the Israelites, as when Elisha's servant sees a previously invisible army of horses and fiery chariots during a siege (2 Kgs 6:17). Other times Yahweh himself marches out from Sinai, Edom, or Seir to battle against Israel's enemies (Deut 33:2–3; Judg 5:4–5; Ps 68:17[E]; Hab 3:3), while numerous other texts simply speak of Yahweh fighting to protect Israel.

Yahweh's protection is also conveyed through the image of a shepherd. Israelites were quite familiar with how a shepherd led the flock to food and water, and protected it from predators such as wolves and lions. This metaphor for Yahweh is reflected in the "name of the Shepherd" used in sequence with "the Mighty One of Jacob" and "the Rock of Israel" in Genesis 49:24. God's role as Israel's Shepherd was often delegated to humans, including tribal leaders, the king, and religious personnel (e.g., Num 27:17; 2 Sam 5:2; 7:7) but they did not always act properly. Thus, in response to the Babylonian conquest of Jerusalem, destruction of the temple, and deportation of many to Babylonia, Second Isaiah, Jeremiah, and Ezekiel each announced that Yahweh would once again shepherd them directly (see, e.g., Isa 40:11; Jer 31:10; Ezek 34:15). Yahweh's divine protection as a shepherd is also celebrated in a number of psalms, most famously in Psalm 23: "The LORD is my Shepherd, I shall not want."

Another divine title is linked to Hagar's encounter with *el roi* ("God who sees") at Beer-Lahai-roi (Gen 16:13–14), which means "well of the Living One who sees." The phrase "the Living God" occurs a number of times throughout the Old Testament (e.g., Deut 5:26; Josh 3:10). This title focuses on God's living, active presence in the lives of both individuals and Israel as a whole.

FAMILY METAPHORS

A final group of divine titles involve family relationships, expressing different degrees of intimacy between God and the people. Just as Israelites are often called God's "children," so God is sometimes called "Father," as in names like Eliab ("My God is Father") and Abijah ("Yahweh is my Father"). God is compared to a father in Psalms 68:5 and 103:13 and is called "Father" directly in Deuteronomy 32:6; Isaiah 63:16; and elsewhere. Building on this, Hosea 11:1–4 describes how Yahweh taught his child Israel/Ephraim to walk just as a loving parent would; God's anguish at the thought of abandoning this child (Hos 11:8–9) is particularly heart wrenching.

In keeping with the ancient belief that every god was either male or female, the male deity Yahweh is never called "Mother," although some texts do compare Israel's God to a mother. Isaiah 49:15 insists that even if a mother forgot the child at her breast or in her womb, Yahweh would never forget Zion. Similarly, in Isaiah 42:14 Yahweh cries out like a woman in labor over the fate of Israel while in Isaiah 66:13 he comforts Israel like a mother comforting her child. Moreover, the Hebrew word for God's compassion in Isaiah 49:15 and 66:13 (and elsewhere) also means "womb." But in stark contrast to these *comparisons*, Deuteronomy 32:18 refers to "the Rock that bore you...the God who gave you birth." We saw above that "the Rock" refers to Yahweh, so this verse describes him as actually giving birth to Israel, which is clearly a mother's role!

There are three other family metaphors for God. God as one's brother, the next of kin who can be relied on to protect and defend one, is found in names like Ahijah ("Yah[weh] is my Brother") and Ahimelech ("My Brother is King"). Similarly, the name Ammiel means "El is my uncle," pointing to a relative who was commissioned to buy back those sold into slavery, reclaim lost land, and so on. Finally, Hosea initiated the concept of Yahweh as Israel's husband (2:16–20 and elsewhere), which was picked up by many later prophets. This emphasized the intimate relationship between Israel and Yahweh when the Israelites were obedient to the commandments, but also allowed for accusations of adultery (e.g., Jer 3:6–10; Ezek 16) when they worshipped other gods.

CONCLUSION

The Old Testament uses many terms and phrases to refer to God, each emphasizing different aspects of God's relationship to Israel. Rather than being a source of confusion, those nuances show that ancient Israel experienced God in different ways. They understood God in hierarchical ways, as lord or king; militaristic ones such as a warrior; familial ones such as father, mother, husband, brother, and uncle; and so on. At the same time, the variation between Yahweh and Elohim in the Pentateuch points to different theological traditions within the first five books of the Bible, which helps explain the sometimes contradictory duplicate stories while also providing even more insight into the different ways Israel understood God over time and in different contexts. Bringing these insights together results in a much richer understanding of the God who is revealed in the Old Testament. Israel did not encounter God solely as an overlord, nor solely as a relative; rather God's very self was revealed in different ways in different contexts. Thus, God does not deal with humans in only one way, but adapts to what the situation requires. This is a valuable lesson for us today as well.

QUESTIONS

1. What are some aspects of God's relationship with Israel that are revealed by the different divine names? Are there insights about God not captured by those names?

2. How does God interact with people today? Is it the same as in the past? How has our understanding of God adapted to the situation of people today?

BIBLIOGRAPHY

Blenkinsopp, Joseph. *The Pentateuch: An Introduction to the First Five Books of the Bible*. Anchor Yale Bible Reference Library. New York: Doubleday, 1992.

Brichto, Herbert Chanan. *The Names of God: Poetic Readings in Biblical Beginnings*. New York: Oxford University Press, 1998.

Campbell, Antony F., and Mark A. O'Brien. *Sources of the Pentateuch: Texts, Introductions, Annotations*. Minneapolis: Fortress Press, 1993.

Clements, Ronald E. "Monotheism and the God of Many Names." In *The God of Israel*, edited by Robert P. Gordon. University of Cambridge Oriental Publications, vol. 64, 47–59. Cambridge: Cambridge University Press, 2007.

Ellis, Peter. *The Yahwist: The Bible's First Theologian*. Collegeville, MN: Liturgical Press, 1968.

Gerstenberger, Erhard S. *Yahweh the Patriarch: Ancient Images of God and Feminist Theology*. Translated by Frederick J. Gaiser. Minneapolis: Fortress Press, 1996.

Lang, Bernhard. "Why God Has So Many Names." *Bible Review* 19, no. 4 (2003): 48–54, 63.

Murphy, Roland E. *Responses to 101 Questions on the Biblical Torah: Reflections on the Pentateuch*. New York / Mahwah, NJ: Paulist Press, 1996.

Chapter 6

WHY LEARN ABOUT BIBLICAL ARCHAEOLOGY?

Leslie J. Hoppe, OFM

READ JOSHUA 6:1—8:29; 10:11–15

CONNECTIONS

There are two channels connecting us to the people of the biblical period. The first is the Bible and other religious literature of ancient Israel, early Judaism, and early Christianity. This literature was the product of elite circles for the most part, that is, people who were literate and had the leisure to produce sophisticated literary and theological works. James Crenshaw maintains that literacy in the Greco-Roman world was about 10 percent, while literacy in ancient Israel was somewhat below this figure. While there have been questions about the accuracy of Crenshaw's statistics, it is clear that most people in ancient Israel and in the Greco-Roman world lived in rural areas and their time was devoted almost entirely to the production, distribution, and preparation of food. They had little opportunity to produce and read the complex literary texts that make up the Bible. Of course, there were the leadership classes: sages, scribes, and priests. It is likely that most books of the Bible were the products of people from these groups.

A second channel connecting us to our religious forebears is made up of the material remains they left behind. These material remains came from people of all social and economic classes, people of various patterns of religious belief and practice, and people of differing political loyalties. The goal of archaeology is to recover these material remains and to determine their significance for understanding the people of antiquity and their culture.

71

A NEW FIELD OF STUDY

Biblical archaeology is a relatively new field of study. Its beginnings can be traced to Old Testament scholars who wished to accomplish for the field of biblical studies what Heinrich Schliemann (1822–90) did for the study of ancient Greek literature. Schliemann was an amateur classicist who wanted to prove that Homer's *Iliad* was an account of a historical event when the virtually unanimous scholarly opinion in the nineteenth century held that the *Iliad* was a work of fiction. Using the geographical information found in Homer, Schliemann began excavations and uncovered a site that he identified as Troy. A few years later, he uncovered the site of Mycenae, the city ruled by Agamemnon, a leader of the Greeks who besieged Troy. Schliemann appeared to be right and the scholars wrong about Homer and the *Iliad*. Schliemann's discoveries led some Old Testament scholars to consider that excavation of sites in the Holy Land might support the historical value of biblical literature, which had come to be suspect with the rise of history as an academic discipline in the middle of the nineteenth century. Many historians of that period assumed that the biblical authors were not eyewitnesses of the events they described, nor did they use eyewitness accounts as they told Israel's story; consequently, one could not accept the Bible as a historical resource.

In 1890, Flinders Petrie (1853–1942), a British Egyptologist, began the first scientific excavation at Tell el-Hesi, a site in the southwest of the Holy Land. ("Tell" is the Arabic word for an artificial mound created by millennia of human occupation.) Petrie recognized the value of pottery for dating and the importance of meticulous recording of the progress of excavation. Since Petrie there has been a continuous procession of biblical scholars, historians, architects, and anthropologists, who have come to the Holy Land in order to engage in the archaeological enterprise. Petrie worked at Hesi for three years. After an interval of nearly eighty years, excavation there began anew in 1970 and continues to the present.

Biblical archaeology, however, has not remained only a scholarly enterprise. People's fascination with the Bible has engendered a fascination with what people of the biblical period left behind. The media have been quick to recognize people's fascination with biblical archaeology. Cable channels regularly run programs, such as *The Naked Archaeologist*, that deal with biblical and ancient Near Eastern archaeology. The readership of *Biblical Archaeology Review* includes more "general" readers than biblical scholars and archaeologists. Googling "biblical archaeology" results in 1.34 million hits.

What does archaeology contribute to our understanding of the Bible and the communities which produced it? The cable TV programs on archaeology focus on the historicity of biblical narratives. So, for example, a program dealing with the Exodus will identify the Pharaoh of the Exodus, offer "scientific" explanations for the ten plagues, and trace the route of the journey from Egypt to Canaan taken by the Hebrew slaves. All this is based on the assumption that the escape of the Hebrew slaves from Egypt was a historical occurrence though only the Bible mentions it. Archaeologists have found no evidence of a mass migration through the Sinai Peninsula at the time the Exodus is assumed to have happened. The word "Exodus" does not appear in the article on the Sinai in the *New Encyclopedia of Archaeological Excavations in the Holy Land*. Still, the eighth-century prophet Hosea assumes that the memory of the Exodus is immensely important for the people of the Kingdom of Israel (see Hos 12:10, 14; 13:4). At present, it is not possible to identify who made up the Exodus group nor can we describe the Exodus experience, but it is clear that the memory of the Exodus was central to the religious beliefs of ancient Israel. There can be a disconnect between the assumptions of the biblical text and the results of archaeology—a disconnect that popular approaches to biblical archaeology often fail to recognize.

Another tack taken by popular approaches to the archaeological enterprise is to focus on controversial questions—often creating a controversy where none exists. Even when responsible biblical scholars appear on programs produced for cable TV, clever editing will make it appear that the scholar gives greater significance to an idiosyncratic hypothesis than it deserves. This is especially true of interpretations of the results of archaeological projects. Stoking the fires of controversy seems to be part of the editorial policy of *Biblical Archaeology Review*. The hype regarding the "Joash stele" and the "James ossuary" had more to do with increasing circulation than shedding light on two "ancient artifacts," which turned out to be forgeries.

The goal of biblical archaeology today is to reconstruct the shape of society in the biblical period through analysis of the material remains uncovered during the course of excavation. This goal is much more comprehensive . than simply determining the history of a site's occupation. Today the methods of excavation and scientific analysis make it possible for archaeologists to be more accurate in plotting out the history of a site's occupation but they also accomplish much more, as they help reconstruct the shape of an ancient society, its religious beliefs, political organization, economic life, even people's diet and health. As the methods of excavation and interpretation became more sophisticated, it became necessary to revise conclusions drawn by earlier projects. The excavations at Jericho and Ai are cases in point.

JERICHO AND AI

Jericho is an oasis found at the southern end of Jordan Valley six miles north of the Dead Sea. People have been living in Jericho's environs for more than nine thousand years, drawn to the area by a freshwater perennial spring that makes possible flourishing agriculture in an otherwise desolate area. A short distance from the spring is the ancient city of Jericho, now known as Tell es-Sultan. According to the Bible, Jericho was the first town captured by the Israelites approaching from the east. Tell es-Sultan was among the sites excavated by the first biblical archaeologists, who sought to use archaeology to support the Bible's reliability as a historical source.

John Garstang (1876–1956), a British archaeologist, dug at Jericho for seven years. He uncovered several mud-brick defensive structures and identified these as the walls that "came tumbling down" during the Israelite attack described in Joshua 6. While Garstang was a skilled archaeologist who recorded his finds with care, excavation techniques were still underdeveloped, leaving the dating of the structures that he discovered to be little more than guesswork. Like many early archaeologists in the Holy Land, Garstang used the Bible to interpret the results of his excavations. These results were considered by many to support the Bible's reliability as a historical source although the circular reasoning involved in such a conclusion is obvious.

A generation later Kathleen Kenyon (1906–78), another British archaeologist, developed more sophisticated excavation techniques that made it possible to date the structures that she found at Jericho with much more precision. She concluded that the walls that Garstang found had been destroyed centuries before the Israelite tribes would have arrived in the vicinity of Jericho. In fact, she maintained that Jericho was abandoned at the time that scholars identified as the period that witnessed the emergence of the Israelites in the land of Canaan. Of course, Kenyon's conclusions caused a storm of controversy, especially among those who were certain that the Book of Joshua provided a historically reliable account of the Israelite "conquest" of Canaan.

In part to help settle this controversy, Joseph Callaway (1920–88) led an excavation project at et-Tell, the site of the biblical city of Ai. According to the Book of Joshua, the Israelites followed their victory at Jericho by moving a few miles westward to attack the city of Ai. They destroyed the city, "reducing it to an everlasting mound of ruins" (Josh 8:28). Callaway assumed that if he could prove that the destruction of Ai took place at the time of the Israelite "conquest," he could support those who assumed that Kenyon's dating of the destruction of Jericho's walls was flawed. After six years of digging, Callaway concluded that Ai was destroyed about a thousand years before the Israelite tribes appeared in Canaan. Archaeology did not support the biblical narratives found in Joshua 6–8.

HAZOR, MEGIDDO, AND JERUSALEM

The results of excavations elsewhere in the Holy Land appeared to have different results. For example, the Israeli archaeologist, Yigael Yadin

(1917–84), led an excavation project at Hazor in northern Israel, and concluded that the ancient city was destroyed by fire in the middle of the thirteenth century BC. Yadin was certain that the destruction layer he uncovered was the result of the Israelite attack related in the Book of Joshua (10:11–15). Yadin also excavated at Megiddo and uncovered stables and gates, which he identified as built by Solomon as part of his construction projects at several cities of his kingdom (see 1 Kgs 9:15). However, subsequent excavations have shown that Yadin's dating of several of the structures he claimed to be Solomonic actually date to the time of King Ahab, who ruled the Kingdom of Israel about a hundred years after Solomon. Hazor is now undergoing re-excavation. One goal of the work at Hazor is to evaluate Yadin's dating of the city's destruction, using techniques of interpretation that are more sophisticated than those available to Yadin. Recent excavations at sites such as Hazor and Megiddo have added support for those historians who maintain that the biblical accounts of the reigns of David and Solomon were not historical but ideological constructions and that the two Israelite national states came into existence no earlier than the ninth century. These historians claim that David and Solomon were, at most, local chieftains rather than rulers of an ancient Near Eastern empire that extended from Dan to Beersheva in Israel and who controlled portions of Syria approaching the Euphrates River, as well as part of the Transjordan, from their capital in Jerusalem.

The dream of every biblical archaeologist is to excavate the city that the Bible claims to be the capital of David's empire. But excavating in Jerusalem brings with it unique problems. First, the modern city is home to almost 800,000 people, most of whom object to being displaced because of excavation projects. Second, some Jews and Muslims object to excavation of certain sites—especially those considered holy places. No excavation is permitted on the *Haram es-Sharif* where two Muslim shrines now stand where the temple was once located. Originally the city of Jerusalem was located on the Ophel, a small hill just south of the walls of the present Old City. Excavations there have not revealed evidence of the city's status as the religious, administrative, and political capital of an empire. This had led some to suggest that the description of the nature and extent of David's kingdom was the product of later propagandists. Indeed, a few historians have claimed that David was not a historical figure simply because no indisputable archaeological evidence for him is available.

In 1993, however, a fragment of inscribed stone was found during excavations at Tel Dan in the north of Israel. Apparently the inscription celebrated the victory of an Aramean king over Israel and "the house of David," a phrase that refers to the dynasty the Bible asserts was established by David. Most scholars acknowledge that this inscription from the ninth century BC is an authentic reference to King David of the Bible. The discovery of the "house of David" inscription illustrates how tentative judgments about the

historical value of some biblical traditions need to be and how archaeology
can require revision of long-held assumptions. An axiom guiding the work of
excavators is "the answer lies below." The solution to problems faced by historians of ancient Israel may yet be uncovered by archaeologists. It is simply
impossible to know. This is the nature of archaeological discovery—one can
never know what may be uncovered in the course of excavation.

ARCHAEOLOGY'S INDEPENDENCE
FROM BIBLICAL STUDIES

The results of excavations reveal the ambiguities that result from
attempting to use archaeology to support the Bible as a reliable historical
source for reconstructing the history of Israel. This has led to a reexamination
of the relationship between biblical studies and archaeology. An approach to
biblical interpretations that has been very influential—especially in the
United States—claims that the Bible presents a "God who acts" in history.
There were certain extraordinary events in the life of the ancient Israelites
which serve as the self-manifestation of the Divine. Of all these, the most
central is the Exodus-Sinai complex of events. In the course of these events,
God was revealed to the Hebrew slaves and biblical faith was born and given
its fundamental form. G. Ernest Wright, a most influential and prolific expo-
nent of this approach, maintained that for biblical faith everything depends
upon whether the central events narrated in the Bible actually occurred. The
results of excavations, however, have made it increasingly more difficult to
maintain that it is possible to reconstruct the history of ancient Israel from
the Bible. Archaeology has led to undermining the historicity of significant
portions of the Scriptures, including the stories about Abraham and Jacob,
the Exodus, the conquest of Canaan, and the early monarchy, though early
archaeological projects in the Holy Land were undertaken precisely to
demonstrate that events narrated in the Bible actually happened.

For a long time, the goals of biblical archaeology were determined by
the agenda and concerns of the biblical text and its interpreters. The one
benefit of archaeology's failure to confirm the historical reliability of biblical
narratives is that archaeology is free to broaden its horizons beyond monumental structures, gates and walls, and the occupational history of sites.
Archaeology's greatest contribution to humanistic studies is its potential for
recreating the world of antiquity on the basis of material remains.
Archaeologists can refocus their energies on what the material remains of
antiquity reveal about the people, their society, and their culture by analysis
of the artifacts that they have uncovered. One example of such work is
"household archaeology," which studies what archaeology can reveal about
the daily lives of ordinary people. To accomplish this, archaeologists will have

to use social-scientific models to understand what their finds can tell them about ancient Israelite society.

The work of Carol Meyers (1942–) illustrates what can be achieved when archaeologists move from their preoccupation with monumental structures and the occupational history of sites to attempt to understand the lives of ordinary folk. Meyers is a leading expert in the study of women in the biblical world. Because of her field experience as a co-director of several archaeological projects in Galilee, she is especially aware of the potential of archaeology to shed light on the role and status of women in ancient Israelite society. She has shown that ordinary women were not powerless in a patriarchal world, but, for example, their role as bakers of bread, the staple of ancient Israelite diet, gave them remarkable control over those whom they fed. She asserts that the social world of ancient Israel was much more complex than a surface reading of the Bible may suggest and that careful study of the data—including archaeological data—may "contest the model of male-dominated hierarchies in premodern societies."

Meyers' work has shown the potential of archaeology to broaden our understanding of the ancient world. Archaeology has the potential for providing the kind of data that can create a more complete portrait of ancient society since archaeology uncovers the material remains of antiquity, remains of people from all classes—those with economic power, political influence, religious insight, and those without. To achieve archaeology's potential for illuminating the shape of ancient society, archaeologists will have to broaden the horizons of their projects beyond looking for monumental structures and give attention to the dwellings of simple peasants.

Today archaeologists who excavate in the Holy Land have more comprehensive and humanistic goals than did some of the early biblical archaeologists. William G. Dever (1933–) has urged archaeological colleagues to broaden their horizons, claiming that with biblical studies setting the agenda, archaeology's accomplishments will be unnecessarily limited. He saw the goal of archaeology as nothing less than the elucidation of the cultural process and asserted that it is necessary to abandon the term "biblical archaeology" in favor of "Syro-Palestinian archaeology" to ensure that archaeology becomes a field of study in its own right—completely independent of biblical studies. Dever also called for professionalization of the practitioners of the discipline: that is, archaeology ought not to be a sideline of biblical scholars but archaeologists need to be trained specifically in their field of study. The archaeological enterprise has changed over the last forty years and Dever's vision for the future of the discipline has begun to take shape.

The results of excavations in the Holy Land have given new direction to writing the history of ancient Israel. The standard histories of Israel often are little more than paraphrases of the biblical narratives. More recent histories such as that of Gösta Ahlström necessarily pay much more attention to the results of archaeological work. Similarly, important commentaries have been written that contain virtually no reference to any archaeological work relevant to the book that is the subject of the commentary. Today that is becoming increasingly less the case. Interpretation of the biblical text ought not take place without some awareness of the results of excavations that can shed light on the cultural context out of which the book emerged.

THE TASK OF INTERPRETATION

The goal of archaeology is not so much to reconstruct the history of Israel or prove the reliability of the Bible as a source in reconstructing that history. Archaeology serves to put us in contact with the people who first heard or read what we now know as the Bible so that we can understand who they were, what their society and its economy and politics were like, what people's concerns and anxieties were, what people ate and how they died— all this so that they can be authentic dialogue partners with people today. Accomplishing this is a not a simple matter. The meaning and significance of the material remains from antiquity require interpretation.

The interpretation of finds uncovered in the course of excavation is the most challenging part of the archaeological enterprise because science and technology have made it possible to recover much more data than ever before. But before interpretation can go forward, it is necessary that excavators publish the results of their field work promptly and completely—something that they have not always done. Until recently, the results of almost half of excavations that were undertaken in the borders of the modern State of Israel have yet to be published. Such publication needs to go beyond providing the raw data uncovered in the course of excavation to the interpretation of the significance of these data by looking for regional patterns, for unique phenomena, for similarities and differences with the results from the data uncovered in other projects. The final report should profile the people who occupied the site at various periods, describing as much of their life, values, work, and culture as possible.

The archaeologist has to be involved in the interpretive task as much as the scholar who focuses on texts. The meaning of a text is not immediately self-evident. Over the last century, biblical scholars have developed a variety of interpretive methods to make it possible for the text to speak to contemporary readers. Similarly in that same period the techniques of excavation and interpretation of archaeological data have become increasingly more sophisticated. Still, the careful use of the most sophisticated methods does not guarantee results that lead to a consensus among archaeologists. Controversies about the origins and shape of the Israelite monarchy and national states testify to that. Archaeologists can look at the same pottery assemblage and be unable to agree on its dating just as two biblical scholars can look at the same text, employing the same basic methodology but arrive at very different conclusions. People often find the disagreements of scholars to be disconcerting. Still, these disagreements reflect the complexity of the interpretive process. Consensus is not easy to achieve. Even when consensus has been reached, often it begins to unravel after time. All this shows the vitality of the interpretive process. As an academic discipline, biblical archaeology is still young, but the achievements and controversies in the field give evidence of its growing maturity.

Today the results of biblical archaeology have led to the rise of two groups of scholars who differ markedly in their interpretation of archaeological discoveries. These two have become known as the "maximalists" and "minimalists." The latter assert that some biblical scholars and historians of ancient Israel (the maximalists) have interpreted archaeology of the Holy Land in light of the Bible, assuming that the Bible recounted the events of ancient Israel's history accurately. The minimalists see the Bible's account of ancient Israel's history as a literary construct that does not reflect historical reality. These two approaches to the interpretation of the results of archaeological work in the Holy Land make it clear that the interpretive task is the most difficult and controversial aspect of any archaeological project. While some of the claims made by the minimalists may be exaggerated, it is no longer possible to excavate with a spade in one hand and the Bible in the other. The Bible can only be used in the interpretation of archaeological data with the utmost care and circumspection.

ARCHAEOLOGY AND EARLY JUDAISM AND EARLY CHRISTIANITY

At one time, scholars thought that it was not necessary to employ archaeology to illuminate the era that witnessed the rise of early Judaism and early Christianity. They assumed that the number and quality of written records from the period provided sufficient information to understand the development of these two religious traditions. Most of the early archaeologists focused their attention almost entirely on sites related to the Hebrew Bible. Few bothered with sites connected to the Christian Scriptures since the question of historicity was framed differently in relationship to that body of texts. No historian questions the existence of Jesus or Paul. Also, the historical period reflected in the New Testament was much shorter than that covered by the Old Testament and was illumined by a wealth of contemporary secular and religious literature. Finally, many scholars located the principal contribution of the New Testament in the area of theology so it was thought that archaeology had little or nothing to contribute to illuminating the theological affirmations of the Christian Scriptures.

Interpreters of the New Testament also have recognized that a purely text-centered approach to biblical interpretation is no longer adequate. Books like Jonathan L. Reed's *Archaeology and the Galilean Jesus* (Harrisburg, PA: Trinity, 2000), his *Excavating Jesus*, written with John Dominic Crossan (San Francisco: HarperCollins, 2002), James H. Charlesworth's *Jesus within Judaism* (NY: Doubleday, 1988), and Marianne Sawicki's *Crossing Galilee* (Harrisburg, PA: Trinity, 2000) show the possibilities of an exegesis that is informed by a knowledge of the social world of early Roman-period Palestine—knowledge made possible, in some measure, with the help of archaeology. One result of excavations of sites in Galilee, for example, called into question the commonly held view that the Jews of Galilee were assimilated into Greco-Roman culture and were less observant than their coreligionists in Judah. Excavations revealed vital Jewish communities that expended a significant amount of their resources to build synagogues in which they could worship their God and strengthen their attachment to their ancestral religion. Perhaps the most tangible evidence of this was the discovery of the Torah shrine of the synagogue of Nabratein in Upper Galilee. At the same time, excavations revealed a diversity of religious expression. For example, the synagogue in nearby Meiron was without any decoration except for geometric patterns while the synagogue at Nabratein displayed architectural elements decorated with floral and animal motifs. Located within a few miles of one another, two Jewish communities had different sensitivities about the appropriateness of images as decorative elements in synagogues even though one of the commandments forbade the production of images.

Archaeology of sites from the time that Judaism and Christianity were developing their distinct identities in Roman Palestine has challenged long-held views based in part on the number and availability of written sources from this period. The most recent of these finds challenges the view that the renovation and expansion of the area surrounding Jerusalem's temple was completed during the reign of Herod the Great. The last surviving portion of Herod's construction is the Western Wall, and the large worked stones at the base of this wall have been called "Herodian stones." The excavation of the street that ran adjacent to the Western Wall, which ancient pilgrims traversed on their way to the temple, yielded ceramics and coins that made it clear that the Western Wall was not completed until at least twenty years after the death of Herod the Great.

One problem regarding early Christianity that archaeology has not been entirely successful in solving is the continued presence of a Jewish Christian community in Palestine after the fall of Jerusalem in AD 70. Writing in the fourth century AD, Eusebius, a church historian, claims that the Jewish-Christian community left Jerusalem during the First Jewish Revolt against Rome (*Histl. eccl.* 3.5.3) for Pella, a city five miles east of the Jordan River and thirty-two miles south of the Sea of Galilee. This journey was supposedly taken in obedience to the command of Christ to "flee to the mountains" when Jerusalem will be desecrated (see Mark 13:3–37). A Franciscan archaeologist, Bellarmino Bagatti (1905–90), argued that there was a continuous Jewish-Christian community in the Holy Land until that community was absorbed into the dominant Byzantine Christian community in the fourth century. Bagatti presents the history and archaeology of those he calls "Judaeo-Christians" in his *The Church from the Circumcision* (Jerusalem: Franciscan Printing Press, 1971). Bagatti's thesis has not won wide support primarily because the archaeological evidence that he presents is open to interpretation that differs widely from that which Bagatti gives. The problem is that Christianity did not develop a symbol system distinct from Judaism in the Holy Land until the Byzantine period. From the perspective of material culture, Jewish Christians are practically indistinguishable from orthodox Jews. In fact, if one had only the archaeological record, one would conclude that Christianity was imported into Palestine in the fourth century. Providing a clear profile of the Jewish-Christian community may be a challenge that archaeology will not meet because of the type of data that one can expect from excavation. Still, one cannot predict what excavation will one day discover.

An example of the unpredictability of archaeological discoveries is the excavation of the synagogue at Capernaum, a site along the northwestern shore of the Sea of Galilee. Jesus made Capernaum the center of his Galilean ministry (Matt 4:13). The New Testament identifies the town's synagogue as the site of an exorcism effected by Jesus (Luke 4:31–37) and the setting for the "bread of life" discourse found in the Fourth Gospel (John 6:59). Remains of an ancient synagogue were visible at the long-abandoned site of Capernaum. Believing those architectural fragments belonged to the building in which Jesus preached, the Franciscan Custody of the Holy Land acquired the site in 1894. Today no one accepts a first-century date for the synagogue, which was excavated and partially rebuilt in the 1920s. Most scholars dated the Capernaum synagogue to the second century because it was a basilica (a rectangular building whose interior space is divided into a central nave and two side aisles by rows of columns) and supposedly this form was typical for synagogues at that time. In 1976, two Franciscan archaeologists, Virgilio Corbo (1918–91) and Stanislao Loffreda (1932–) took up pavers that covered the synagogue's floor and discovered thousands of coins from the late-fourth century AD. This led them to date the synagogue to the late-fourth or early-fifth century. Proponents of the second-century dating suggested that building such a magnificent structure as the Capernaum synagogue in the fourth or fifth centuries would have been impossible since the laws of the Byzantine Empire forbade building or repairing of synagogues. That such a magnificent structure was, in fact, built suggests that the Christians and Jews of Capernaum must have disregarded imperial law for the sake of maintaining good relations. The dating for the Capernaum synagogue suggested by the work of Corbo and Loffreda has been supported by analysis of the capitals that graced the columns of the synagogue. Though the Byzantine emperors did promulgate anti-Jewish laws, Capernaum offers one example of how those laws were ignored so that a very impressive and beautiful house of prayer was built to accommodate the Jewish community of the town. We would never have known of this apart from the archaeological work, which was originally intended to shore up evidence for the second-century AD date of the synagogue. Again—the answers lie below.

CONCLUSION: THE CONTRIBUTION
OF BIBLICAL ARCHAEOLOGY

The goals of those who produced biblical literature were religious in nature. The biblical authors were not at all concerned with providing a complete and objective profile of their society's politics, religion, economy, art and architecture, settlement patterns, and the like. They simply assumed a familiarity with these. Readers today who look for information about ancient Israelite and Greco-Roman society from the books of the Bible will find, at best, an incomplete and somewhat random picture. One goal of biblical archaeology is to fill out that picture so that we can understand the people of the biblical period—their values, their culture, their society, their religious beliefs and practices—on the basis of the material remains they left behind. This will enable us to better understand and appreciate the literary remains left by those same people. It enables us to read the Bible in its cultural setting.

Archaeology of the Holy Land gives us a connection with our religious forebears, Jewish and Christian. American culture tends to view religious commitment as something personal and private—a matter between the individual and God. Archaeology makes it possible to experience how belief helped shape the lives of the people of antiquity, who were committed to passing on their religious traditions and beliefs to succeeding generations. While the Bible presents the content of Jewish and Christian religious tradition, archaeology enables people today to see those traditions as a living reality, shaping the lives of ordinary folk. Confessing Christian traditions such as Catholicism have a high regard for doctrinal orthodoxy. The Church has a long theological tradition, demonstrating how seriously people of faith have taken the matter of religious belief. The problem that comes with the

Church's theological traditions is that faith can become an abstraction. Archaeology can help prevent that from happening.

Biblical archaeology today has freed itself from a preoccupation with history and the best excavation projects have wide cultural horizons. Archaeology is less concerned with the occupational history of a site than it is with those who occupied the site and their society, political system, economy, values, diet, health, aesthetics—everything that helps us understand who they were and how they mastered life. Some people look for archaeology to "prove" the Bible's historical value, its trustworthiness, even its revelatory character. But archaeology has nothing to prove. It is a humanistic science— a science about people. Archaeology is an important partner—along with the Bible—in making possible an authentic encounter between believers today and their ancestors in the faith.

QUESTIONS

1. What can biblical archaeology tell us about the world of the Bible that the Scriptures do not?

2. Why are so many people interested in biblical archaeology?

3. What are the challenges that biblical archaeology faces as it studies the world of antiquity?

BIBLIOGRAPHY

Ahlström, Gösta. *History of Ancient Palestine*. Minneapolis: Fortress Press, 1993.

Crenshaw, James. *Education in Ancient Israel: Across the Deadening Silence*. Anchor Bible Reference Library. New York: Doubleday, 1998.

Davis, Thomas W. *Sifting Sands: The Rise and Fall of Biblical Archaeology*. New York: Oxford University Press, 2004.

Dever, William G. *What Did the Biblical Writers Know and When Did They Know It? What Archaeology Can Tell Us about the Reality of Ancient Israel*. Grand Rapids, MI: Eerdmans, 2001.

Finkelstein, Israel. *David and Solomon: In Search of the Bible's Sacred Kings and the Roots of the Western Tradition*. New York: Free Press, 2006.

Frendo, Anthony J. *Pre-Exilic Israel, the Hebrew Bible and Archaeology: Integrating Text and Artefact*. London: T&T Clark, 2011.

Fritz, Volkmar. *An Introduction to Biblical Archaeology*. Sheffield, England: JSOT Press, 1994.

Hoppe, Leslie J., OFM. *What Are They Saying about Biblical Archaeology?* New York / Mahwah, NJ: Paulist Press, 1984.

Meyers, Carol. "From Field Crops to Food." *Annual of the American Schools of Oriental Research* 60/61 (2006–7): 67–84.

Rast, Walter E. *Through the Ages in Palestinian Archaeology: An Introductory Handbook.* Philadelphia: Trinity, 1992.

Wright, G. Ernest. *God Who Acts: Biblical Theology as Recital.* London: SCM, 1952.

Chapter 7

WHY IS A LOVING GOD SO ANGRY IN THE BIBLE?

Mark S. Smith

READ LAMENTATIONS 1–2

When I teach the Old Testament, the wrath of God is one of the biggest problems that my students have with this part of the Bible. At times, divine anger can seem incomprehensible to readers of the Bible. Even when it is understood to be the divine punishment, divine wrath can seem excessive, as it did to the author of Lamentations: "How the Lord in his anger has humiliated daughter Zion" (2:1). This chapter continues with its depiction of divine anger; it even calls the Lord "ruthless" (2:20) and "without pity" (2:21). Ezekiel 16 goes further in its description of Israel as a prostitute. As punishment for her sins, God promises to gather her former "lovers" (the other nations) to strip her and to stone her and to hack her into pieces (vv. 35–43). The same passage shows God promising: "I will…bring blood upon you in wrath and jealousy" (v. 38). The savage description here borders on the pornographic, and it seems impossible for, if not unworthy of, a loving God. As a result of such passages, students often think of the biblical God as a divine judge waiting for them to make mistakes and then to punish them. As a result, when it comes to the God of the Bible, divine anger looms large in their imaginations, and they find it hard to read about God in the Bible. Their sense of Jesus partially alleviates this idea of the divine judge. Their assumption is that Jesus overcomes this otherwise negative picture of God, but then they are inclined to skip over most parts of the Old Testament (except for the stories in Genesis and some of the psalms—they like those parts.) But on the whole, God as represented in the Old Testament (or God the Father) is often not really God for them. The pattern of divine judgment and punishment,

85

often accompanied by divine anger and wrath, does not seem like God for them. So how could it be in the Bible?

Divine anger and wrath simply seem unfathomable for a loving and good God. By comparison, readers have no trouble with biblical expressions of God's love. Across the pages of the Scriptures, God voices divine love for Israel (Deut 7:8, 13; 23:6; Hos 3:1; 9:15; 11:1; 14:5; 1 Kgs 10:9; 2 Chr 2:10; 9:8; Ps 47:5; Isa 43:4; 48:14; Jer 31:3; Mal 1:2). Divine love is also expressed for specific people, such as "the ancestors" (Deut 4:37) and Solomon (2 Sam 12:24; Neh 13:26). God loves "the righteous" (Ps 146:9), those who accept divine discipline (Prov 3:12), and the "one who pursues justice" (Prov 15:9). Yet divine anger and wrath are no less present in passages of the Bible. Wrath is a common divine response to past sin (2 Kgs 22:13, 17). Divine anger and wrath vented against Israel is held up as the divine punishment for idolatry if Israel does not turn from its sins (see Deut 29:21–27; Jer 4:1–4). In these cases, the threat of divine anger is designed to motivate Israel not to sin.

Many people think that divine anger is the primary way that the Bible—and especially the Old Testament—understands God. Sometimes this is because they learned the mistaken notion that the God of the Old Testament is a God of judgment and wrath but that the God of the New Testament is a God of love (for example, in the commandment to love one's enemies in Matt 5:44; Luke 6:27). It is true that the God of the New Testament is a God of love (as God is in the Old Testament), but judgment and love are attributed to God in both testaments. The New Testament refers to divine wrath in many places. The "wrath of God" is upon those who disobey Jesus, in John 3:36. According to Romans 1:18, "the wrath of God is revealed from heaven against all ungodliness and wickedness of those who by their wickedness suppress the truth." Ephesians 5:6 similarly proclaims that "the wrath of God comes on those who are disobedient" (see also Col 3:6). These are not isolated expressions (see the expressions of divine wrath in Rom 2:5; 3:5; 9:22; 12:19; 13:4–5; 1 Thess 1:10; Rev 6:16–17; 11:18; 16:19). God is a force of violent judgment, according to Matthew 13:41–43, 49; 18:34–35. Jesus, too, is a source of violence: "Do not think that I have come to bring peace upon the earth. I have come to bring not peace but the sword" (Matt 10:34). Jesus also issues words of woe against towns that do not accept him (Matt 11:20–24). Jesus even curses a tree, even though "it was not the time for figs" (Mark 11:12–14, 20–21; Matt 21:18–19). So we can see that the New Testament contains many expressions of divine wrath and punishment. When we consider these passages from the New Testament, it is impossible to view the God of the Old Testament as a God of wrath in contrast to the God of the New Testament as a God of love. Both testaments show God as a God of love and of anger, and for Christians this is the same God. God's love for us and God's violent anger seem totally opposite, and yet for the Bible they are two sides of the same God.

Part of the answer is that this view of divine anger is not quite fair to God in either the Old or New Testament. The understanding of God is more complex. Indeed, this understanding of divine anger and love is itself not biblical. Up to this point, we have discussed divine love and anger in the Bible as if they were polar opposites. It is assumed by many modern readers that love and anger have nothing to do with one another. Today people have particular trouble with the emotion of anger. Anger is a very tough emotion. It reeks of personal abuse and violence. In people's imaginations, anger does not seem too distant from hate, and everyone is, of course, against hate. When we turn to the Bible and see divine anger expressed on its pages, we may be repulsed by it. A God worthy of our devotion, it would seem, is a God who loves us and is certainly not an angry God. However, this is a relatively modern idea. It is certainly not a biblical view of love and anger, whether human or divine.

In a probing article entitled "The Beauty of the Bloody God," the biblical scholar Corrinne Carvalho asks: "Are we the devil?" She then offers her reflections on the problem as she sees it:

> Are some descriptions of violence always evil? Always beautiful? Certainly not. Violent images can simply be inflammatory, disgusting, and gratuitous. I would argue that language about violence, just like descriptions of sexual activity, are not inherently good or bad; erotic or pornographic; glorious or gory. Rather, violent images can be used to resist, recover, entertain, inflame or inspire. Therefore, while some violent texts provide an outlet for human violence or function as a therapeutic outlet for victims of violence, sometimes they provide an aesthetic experience. Are they beautiful? That would depend on one's definition of "beautiful." However, I do know that for many readers these texts are moving, memorable, complex, fascinating, emotive, satisfying, and an appropriate revelatory experience of God.

Biblical representations of the violent God are complex, and they cannot simply be labeled as bad because they are violent. In Carvalho's view, that's too simplistic. Instead, our understanding needs to be open-ended in our trying to understand God, especially considering our own human limitations. Carvalho seems to understand that images of the violent and angry God suffer in their limitations by human nature, yet capture helpful dimensions of what the divine is all about. Carvalho ends her reflections in this way: "We can't get rid of sex or violence and remain human, and we can't remain human without misusing them. We remain on this side of reality where the grotesque is beautiful." The violence of God in the Bible is a significant problem, yet for us today, it is also a significant opportunity to set aside for a moment our own assumptions and ways of thinking and to ask instead what the sort of thinking was for ancient Israelites and how this might help us understand the biblical God anew. My goal here is not to "defend" or justify divine anger in modern terms (I don't think anger is defensible), but to understand it in its biblical terms. The authors of the Scriptures did not view divine love and divine anger as entirely opposite emotions but as related emotions. And they also did not view them simply as emotions, but as sets of behaviors. At this point, I am going to try to explain how love and anger are related in the Bible. I don't think that this will make readers feel any better about divine anger, but it may make it more understandable; and it might even be possible to recast or "translate" biblical anger in a way that still reflects the biblical witness to who God is, and can be, for us.

While the emotions of love and anger seem contradictory in our cultural context, the ancient writers of the Scriptures did not share this view. In Israel's own religious context, divine love represented God's recognition of human fidelity to the covenantal relationship with God, while divine anger aimed at Israelites commonly resulted from their failure to keep their covenant relationship with God. In other words, God shows love to those who keep the covenant and anger to those who don't. Divine love and anger are two sides of the same covenant relationship. While we do not need to adopt this view just because it is in the Scriptures, we do need to understand it in order to see why the ancient writers would attribute such a seemingly negative emotion to a good and loving God. The Bible does not represent love and anger as antithetical or opposites. At a very fundamental level, anger of God and love of God in the Bible are intricately related. So this is a beginning point for understanding divine anger, but we can go further.

To understand divine anger in the Bible better, we need to know a little about human anger in ancient Israel. Human anger is the model for divine anger, and while there may be some differences between them, looking first at human anger will help give further perspective on divine anger. Human anger is considered a natural human response to danger, whether an offense to oneself or to others of concern. As Deena Grant has shown in her work (which I have drawn on extensively here for this discussion), biblical anger most commonly arises in contexts of struggle for authority and it is expressed by positions of authority, especially by fathers and kings. Of the twenty-six individuals named in the Bible who express anger, twenty-one are kings, leaders, masters, or high-ranking family members. Esau gets angry at his younger brother for stealing his birthright (Gen 27:45). Moses' anger is directed at Korah, Dothan, and Abiram for their rebellion against his authority (Num 16:15). In the story of Esther, the wicked Haman gets furious over Mordecai's refusal to bow to him. In these and many other passages, people manifest their anger when they perceive that someone of lesser social rank has violated their authority. Even the two passages where a subordinate does appear to get angry at a superior are quite telling. These are Jonathan's anger when he discovers Saul's intent to kill David (1 Sam 20:34), and David's anger over God's execution of Uzzah (2 Sam 6:8). Even in these cases, the Bible seems to avoid describing the subordinate as angry at his superior; instead, they describe the angry parties as angry at the situation.

Typically, anger is often expressed in meeting challenges from outside of the family unit; anger is the emotion shown to defend the family. So they try to kill or banish people that threaten the family. The brothers of Dinah kill Shechem and all the males of his town (Gen 39:19–20). In contrast, a father's anger at family members is almost never lethal. Saul throws a spear at Jonathan (1 Sam 20), but Jonathan escapes unharmed. In fact, anger at family members often incurs no punishment at all. Paternal anger is almost always benign (1 Sam 20:30–34; 2 Sam 13:21). David gets angry at Amnon for his rape of Tamar (2 Sam 13:21), but David does nothing to him. A husband's anger is likewise not lethal for a perceived offense (Gen 30:2), but a wife may be punished for behavior perceived to be undermining of her husband's authority (Judg 14:19–20; Esth 1:21–22) or if she is suspected of adultery, also a perceived threat to his authority (Num 5). With brothers, the bonds are sometimes represented in similar terms. Esau's anger subsides after he expresses his wish to kill his brother, Jacob (Gen 27:45); indeed, later when they meet, it is Esau who is ready to embrace Jacob (Gen 33:4).

Now let's return to the anger of God. Like human anger, divine anger is often triggered by human disregard of divine authority. The only time God gets angry but does not punish is with Moses. When Moses first refuses God's commission to go to Egypt (Exod 4:14), God gets angry, but he simply offers a way around the problem by suggesting that Moses' brother Aaron go with him. Here God sounds like a father who gets angry but does not punish his son for the affront to his authority; rather, he seeks a solution to the problem. Commonly, God is angered by idolatry (Exod 32:20, the golden calf), or by religious violations, such as breaking the Sabbath (Ezek 20:13), or for cultic purity infractions (Lev 6:1–6). All are infringements on God's authority or presence within Israel. Equally important, divine anger sometimes expresses God's care for others, in some cases in situations of social injustice: "You shall not wrong or oppress a resident alien, for you were aliens in the land of Egypt. You shall not abuse any widow or orphan. If you do abuse them, when they cry out to me, I will surely heed their cry; my wrath will burn, and I will kill you with the sword, and your wives shall become widows and your children orphans" (Exod 22:21–24). Here, God's anger is a statement of God's care for the least of Israel. A comparable motivation informs divine anger against the nations when they assault or oppress Israel (Exod 15:7–8; Jer 50:13; Ezek 25:14).

Biblical metaphors for God show that the model of human interaction informs divine anger, especially when God is compared with a disregarded husband or father (Judg 2:17; Jer 2:2–35; Ezek 6:9–12; 16:7–13; Hos 11:1–9), a property owner who has been robbed (Josh 7:1–26), a defied political leader (Num 11:10–20, 33; Ezek 20:8–38; Zeph 3:7–15), or a spurned covenant partner (Deut 4). In other words, God is characteristically imaged as a father or king when he gets angry. At the same time, the ultimate aim of divine anger is not simply the restoration of divine authority. It is an act of persuasion on God's part, to remind Israel that God is Israel's rightful authority. He is their father, and when he gets angry at Israel as his children, then his anger is ultimately tempered, in contrast with his anger at the nations, which is lethal. The anger of God reminds Israel that Israel belongs to God as family, and his anger against others for the sake of Israel is ultimately an expression of divine love for Israel. The reasons given for divine forgiveness of Israel are related to love in this family: God's affection for Israel, the covenant between them, Israel's repentance, and even God's reputation among the nations.

There is a further dimension of divine anger that is also based on human behavior, and in particular on human aggression. This is considered in ancient cultures to be a prized characteristic, even a virtue, and when it is applied to God, it shows the divine desire and capacity to defend Israel. This warrior aggression is often characterized as "strength, might, fierceness." At its core, this idea is essentially a physical term. When used in the context of conflict, the word may further denote fierceness, which involves the interface of the physical ability and the psychological demeanor. In modern terms, this martial aggression sounds like the physical and psychological effects of adrenaline produced by the "fight or flight" response in the face of a serious threat. Fierceness is the response of readiness and disposition to fight. Some of this aggression appears with the set of terms for divine anger that we have already seen. This anger is associated commonly with the verb, "to burn," grounded in the physical experience of anger in the face (i.e., increase in facial temperature accompanied by an increase in rate of breathing). This "wrath" (Exod 15:7) is also called "the blast of the breath of his nostrils" (2 Sam 22:16/Ps 18:16). It is at once an expression of anger and a bodily response. Yahweh's "anger…wrath…rage" are all manifest in Habakkuk 3:8. God is compared with the warrior and his "fury" in Isaiah 42:13 (cf. Isa 59:17; Ezek 23:25; Pss 76:11 and 79:5–6). God's anger here is based on the model of human warriorship, where this emotion is a prized virtue in "the heat of battle." In the great Greek classic, the *Iliad*, the classic model of this warrior behavior is Achilles with his notorious fury. The very theme of the *Iliad* as stated at its very outset is not the war, or even its heroes, or even the greatest hero, Achilles, but specifically his fury. This is the very first word of the *Iliad*. This anger and fury goes well beyond "strength, fierceness." The basic analogy is a bodily condition of "burning" or "heat." It involves an excess of physical energy directed at a perceived enemy.

The terms involved express an intense martial aggression. Indeed, such aggression may be pursued on the battlefield, as it says in biblical passages, to the point of putting one's own life at grave mortal risk ("scorned death" in Judg 5:18). This anger and fury are channeled for meeting the enemy successfully, and in the Bible this is often on behalf of others. In human fierceness, it is to defend against human enemies; for God, it is to defend against cosmic enemies (Hab 3:10) or to defend Israel against its enemies. More specifically, it is to defend those whom God views as God's own. God is willing to fight for others. In the context of battle, these terms express a positive quality for ancient Israel. To be sure, such aggression on the part of humans could get out of control, which was recognized as a social danger (see Gen 49:6–7; 2 Sam 3:39; cf. Amos 1:11). In the case of divine warriors, this quality too was considered potentially dangerous (Yahweh in Ps 74:1; 2:3–4; 4:11). But when it was directed against enemies, it was a prized quality (Yahweh in Isa 42:13; 3:66).

Divine anger is thus not only to safeguard the divine Father's authority, but also to secure the divine family's well-being. And God may abandon divine anger, especially when it concerns his own family, Ephraim (another term for Israel). In Hosea 11:8, he calls Ephraim "my son" and then asks: "How can I give you up, O Ephraim?…My heart recoils within me; my compassion grows warm and tender. I will not execute my fierce anger; I will not again destroy Ephraim" (Hos 11:8–9). This quote from Hosea may remind us that God's compassion for Israel is understood in association with the fierce anger of God. The ancient context in which such compassion and anger are interrelated responses is the context of a family relationship between two parties. Hosea expresses Yahweh's love for Israel (like a husband for a wife, in 3:1, and like a father for a son, in 11:1). Similarly, the Book of Deuteronomy speaks not only of God's love but also of the imperative necessity of Israel's love in return. Deuteronomy 6 famously commands Israel to love the Lord with all of its self (v. 5), and chapter 11 commands this love specifically in connection with obeying God's laws, rules, and commandments (v. 1). Love of God is not simply a general sense or a feeling. It is a series of practices that demonstrate fidelity. Love of God in Deuteronomy is covenant love, a love "defined by and pledged in the covenant" (Moran; Lapsley).

Many scholars have shown that covenant love binding its parties together corresponds on the human level to human relationships between persons who are not related to one another by blood. Covenant is family substitute. David and Jonathan make a covenant and they share love, as beautifully described in 1 Samuel 18:1: "When David had finished speaking to Saul, the soul of Jonathan was bound to the soul of David, and Jonathan loved him as his own soul" (see also 1 Sam 20:17). Sound familiar? (It is familiar to Christians from the citation of Lev 19:18 in Matt 22:39; Mark 12:31; Luke 11:27.) Kings of relative parity make treaties expressed with love. For example, Hiram king of Tyre is called David's "friend" (1 Kgs 5:15); this word in this case is derived from the verb, "to love." Kings make treaties with vassals, who are required to love them and to perform service and obedience to them. Kings commonly speak of their love for one another and call each other brother (when they are in an a relatively equal relationship) or father (when the relationship is not between relative equals). As noted by William Moran, the king of Assyria required his vassals to take loyalty oaths, and these included the following requirement: "You will love Assurbanipal as yourselves." (Sound familiar?) In another text the oath is recorded: "...the king of Assyria, our lord, we will love." Up and down the social scale, covenant and treaty are means used to establish relationships across kinship lines, and these relationships come with responsibilities. According to Deuteronomy 6:5, such love requires the all of Israel; in context, this meant the Sinai covenant.

So what does love have to do with anger? Divine anger is the representation of divine responses to attacks on Israel as the family of God, or to Israel's own failures to keep the covenant. It is, in Julia O'Brien's words, "a powerful claim of divine concern for human suffering." O'Brien also suggests that the modern reaction against the violence of God of the Bible says more about modern sensitivities than it does about the Bible. Our negative responses to divine anger in the Bible may reflect our own feelings about violence, but they may overlook the message being communicated in the Bible about God's justice or the responsibilities of the covenant, which for the biblical authors comes with real consequences if not met. We can't focus only on the violence and then miss what may be the deeper expression of divine concern in the Bible. At the same time, we shouldn't ignore the violence; we can be critical of it but also think about it and ask how it made for a compelling image of God in biblical times. We can recognize that our times are different from biblical times, and that we do not need to endorse all of its images for God that come from those times. We would not place as much emphasis on male models for God (father, warrior) as the biblical authors did; the Bible may be God's first word to us, but for Catholics, it is hardly the last word. Even as we may be able to—and should—set aside anger both human and divine as biblical models, we do need, however, to understand the deeper meanings and messages that were conveyed by images of divine anger.

Part of the difficulty is that many Americans are largely insulated from violence due to foreign enemies, not infrequently the context for divine anger in the Bible. (This is not to say that Americans don't experience violence; we face an epidemic of domestic abuse and other forms of violence.) The world of the biblical authors experienced invasions and destruction at the hands of enemies, and often their only resort for expressing their hope was to call on God to express divine-warrior anger. This idea was in keeping with traditional expression across the ancient Near East, and so divine anger became part of the Israelites' expression of God, sometimes for expressing divine justice.

We should not be surprised by this kind of thinking. It is one that many find comfort in when it is used of God. Many Christians find consolation in Mary's wonderful psalm of praise known as the Magnificat (Luke 1:46–55). This song includes the exercise of divine might and even violent judgment against the mighty (vv. 51–52), which seems consoling to many readers, especially when they are powerless, precisely because it witnesses to God's aid; it is for God, in the view of this text, to set things right.

When Israel is telling God that Israel does not love God even as God continues to love Israel, God can respond with anger, even with dangerous punishments that so many people think of as typical of God in the Bible. In addition to what I have suggested about the relationship between divine love and anger, I want to note also the Bible offers models for understanding that go beyond divine anger. There are alternative views about punishment within the Bible. For example, according to Psalm 1, the wicked punish themselves by having their way separate from God: ungrounded in the reality of God, they are like chaff that blows away (v. 3), and their way simply perishes, unlike the way of the righteous whom God knows (v. 6). Ezekiel offers a second perspective: Israel rejects God and thus drives God away, leaving Israel vulnerable to attacks by others such as Assyria or Babylonia. More specifically for Ezekiel, Israel's sins made the temple impure, thus driving God into exile (see chapters 8 to 10). We see yet a third model in Jeremiah. In Jeremiah, Israel is regarded as the aggressor against God (Jer 12:7–8):

> I have forsaken my house,
> I have abandoned my heritage,
> I have given the beloved of my heart
> into the hands of her enemies.
> My heritage has become to me
> like a lion in the forest;
> she has lifted up her voice against me—
> therefore I hate her.

Israel is the lion, in short the animalistic aggressor that has acted against God first. My point in mentioning these passages from Psalm 1, Ezekiel, and Jeremiah is to note that there are multiple biblical models for what is going on in the relationship between God and those who reject God; divine wrath is only one of these models. We may think of this model primarily, because this is what we heard as children or perhaps what we could hear as children. But we are no longer children.

There is still more to the story of divine anger in the Bible. Even if God is rejected by Israel, God's anger is not entirely like human anger. God's anger can be swayed by divine mercy (Judg 2:14–18; 3:8–10). Put another way, when God's anger and mercy hang in the balance, divine anger induces human acknowledgment of the need for divine mercy. Divine anger and mercy stand ultimately in a sort of "divine dialogue" within God, as God pursues a dialogue with humanity. In Hosea 11:9 God reminds Israel: "I am God and no mortal." God can relent even when those whom God loves fail: "My heart recoils within me" (Hos 11:8). What is remarkable is that human efforts matter, that they can affect the divine; they can mollify the divine heart. In the words of Yohanan Muffs, "We must consider not only YHWH's love, but also His anger and the human capacity to mollify it." In a sense, divine anger and compassion together express the more basic reality of divine love. God cares; God cares enough to be moved by humanity. In responding with anger against humans, God gets their attention; and as a result they may learn that the effects of their behaviors and their consequences extend beyond their own horizons. And they are responsible. And even when—or especially when—faced with human failure, the heart of God the heavenly Father and warrior weeps, stirred with pity for Israel (Jer 4:19; 8:23; 14:17; 31:20; Hos 11:8–9; Roberts).

QUESTIONS

1. How do you feel about the idea of God as angry? Does this sense of God belong to your idea of God?

2. For you, how does your sense of God as angry and loving fit together?

3. According to the Bible, what are the reasons for God getting angry? What images of God are used in expressing divine anger?

4. How does the Bible put divine anger together with divine love?

5. How does the Bible's way of putting divine love and anger together compare with yours?

6. If there is a difference between the Bible's approach and yours to divine emotions, how might this reflection help you for your prayer?

BIBLIOGRAPHY

Carvalho, Corrine. "The Beauty of the Bloody God: The Divine Warrior in Prophetic Literature." In *Aesthetics of Violence in the Prophets*, edited by Chris Franke and Julia M. O'Brien, 131–52. Library of Hebrew Bible/ Old Testament Studies 515. New York/London: T & T Clark, 2010.

Grant, Deena. "Wrath of God." In *The New Interpreter's Dictionary of the Bible*, edited by Katharine Doob Sakenfeld et al., 5:932–37. Nashville: Abingdon, 2009.

Lapsley, Jacqueline E. "Feeling Our Way: Love for God in Deuteronomy." *Catholic Biblical Quarterly* 65 (2003): 350–69.

Moran, William L. "The Ancient Near Eastern Background of the Love of God in Deuteronomy." *Catholic Biblical Quarterly* 25 (1963): 77–87. Reprinted in Moran, *The Most Magic Word*, edited by Ronald S. Hendel, 170–81. The Catholic Biblical Quarterly Monograph Series 35. Washington, DC: The Catholic Biblical Association of America, 2002. 170–81.

Muffs, Yochanan. "On Biblical Anthropomorphism." In *Bringing the Hidden to Light: The Process of Interpretation. Studies in Honor of Stephen A. Geller*, edited by Kathryn F. Kravitz and Diane M. Sharon, 163–68. Winona Lake, IN: Eisenbrauns, 2007.

O'Brien, Julia M. *Challenging Prophetic Metaphor: Theology and Ideology in the Prophets*. Louisville: Westminster John Knox, 2008.

O'Connor, Kathleen. *Lamentations and the Tears of the World*. Maryknoll, NY: Orbis, 2002.

Roberts, J. J. M. "The Motif of the Weeping God in Jeremiah." In Roberts, *The Bible and the Ancient Near East: Collected Essays*, 132–42. Winona Lake, IN: Eisenbrauns, 2002.

Zenger, Erich, A *God of Vengeance? Understanding the Psalms of Divine Wrath*. Louisville: Westminster John Knox, 1996.

Chapter 8

WHY PRAY THE PSALMS?

Dale Launderville, OSB

READ PSALMS 15, 22, 73, 90, 102, 112

The psalms are good for the heart. When we speak of the "heart" in the Psalter, we are referring to more than the pump for blood. The "heart" (Hebrew, *lēb*, *lēbāb*) is the center from which our thoughts and feelings arise. If someone should tell me, "your heart is in the right place," I am encouraged that another person sees me as one who tries to make judgments that are just and promote the harmony that God intends for the world. Fr. Lawrence Boadt, CSP, was surely a man whose heart was in the right place. He was an accomplished biblical scholar who typically would take theological conversations to a new level of understanding. Furthermore, he demonstrated how well-grounded he was in the mystery of Christ by his passion for communicating the biblical message effectively. One small illustration of his efforts to bring his biblical scholarship to a wider audience is his article "Catholic Evangelization and the Psalms" in the *Josephinum Journal of Theology* 10 (2003): 3–18. We are all deeply indebted to this generous man of faith who showed us how the Word of God is a never-ending source of nourishment. In this essay in his honor, I will gather together the verses in which the word "heart" is used in the psalms and discuss how their message can help us to pray the psalms so that our hearts might be in the right place with God.

WHAT IS PRAYER?

Most of us were taught the Our Father, the Hail Mary, and the Glory Be by our parents and teachers. Nevertheless, we know well the truth of St. Paul's statement: "We do not know how to pray as we ought" (Rom 8:26). A

major resource for learning how to pray over the past two millennia has been
the Psalter. Jewish and Christian believers have recited its hymns, complaints, and thanksgivings in order to communicate honestly and openly with
God about what is happening in their lives. The psalms offer words for many
of the feelings and thoughts that rise up within us at important times in our
relationship with God and with other humans. The psalms put these important moments into the framework of the wisdom of the ancestors that is oth
erwise narrated in the stories and teachings of the Old Testament. The
psalms help us to connect our stories with the stories of our ancestors in the
faith and do so primarily by bringing us into conversation with God—a conversation that sustained those who have gone before us in the faith. The
psalms help us to come to know God as a trusted authority and friend who
will walk along with us and guide us to new life. In the psalms, God gives us
these words of prayer so that he might listen to us. He gives us the opportunity to talk about what is troubling us or is uppermost in our minds. This conversation helps us to keep in perspective the dangers that threaten our lives
and to trust that God will care for us. The psalms help us to realize that we
can only be happy if God is with us and sustaining our hearts.

WHY PRAYING THE PSALMS CAN BRING US NEW LIFE

The goal of knowing God includes within it the objective of coming into
communion with all of reality. Such "right-wising" of our relationship with
God and all of creation is illustrated in the exuberant thanksgiving that concludes Psalm 22 (vv. 22–32). When the petitioner becomes aware that God
intends to heal and save him from the hostility of the foes, the petitioner proclaims this good news to the assembled worshippers and concludes with the
wish: "May your hearts continue in life forever!" (v. 26b; all translations are
my own in order to emphasize consistently the body language of "heart,"
since other translations render the Hebrew word *lēb* as "mind" or "will" in
particular contexts). The overflowing joy of the healed petitioner leads this
person to wish enduring and abundant life to those round about. But remarkably, this joyful one then goes on to proclaim that all nations and their rulers,
all those who have died, and all those yet to be born will acknowledge the saving power of God and bow down in worship. This expectation of the communion of all humans through all generations, as expressed in the Zion
tradition (Isa 2:2–5; 60:1–16), is concretized in the particular experience of
the healed petitioner. The drama of the healed one's proclamation echoes in
quieter ways throughout the Psalter where we see the reality of coming into
communion with God and others as the goal of our striving.

A ritual commonly experienced by pilgrims to Jerusalem was the
entrance rite to the temple court as articulated in Psalms 15 and 24. Psalm

24:4 speaks of those who are "pure of heart" as worthy to enter into sacred space; they have kept themselves from worshipping idols—that is, of allowing anything to displace God's centrality in their concerns. Psalm 15:2 refers to those who characteristically "speak the truth from the heart." The integrity required for entering before the Lord and proclaiming one's adherence to God's person and teaching demanded that one be honest and caring in one's dealings with others as well as being one who honors the Lord. The opposite of such a person of integrity was the one who has a "crooked heart" (Ps 101:4). The king who speaks in Psalm 101 finds that the one who takes the pathway of the arrogant (Ps 101:5) acts perversely and so must be removed from the city of the Lord (Ps 101:8). This teaching on the two ways pervades the Psalter and emphasizes that the human agent has a key role in shaping the journey toward communion with God and others.

The pilgrim's journey to God is an immersion experience. Going up to Jerusalem has a physical as well as an emotional dimension. In many psalms, the pray-er suffers a loss of vitality from illness or the hostility of foes. In Psalm 102:4, the afflicted petitioner cries out: "My heart is attacked, dried up like grass." In Psalm 22:14, the anxious petitioner responds to threatening, animal-like foes by complaining, "my heart has become like wax; it is melted within me." More than one-quarter of the psalms take the form of individual complaints, of which the majority are concentrated in the first two books of the Psalter. An advantage of this editorial arrangement is that it allows the diverse articulations of human brokenness in the psalms to be available to the pray-er in the first part of the Psalter and thereby increases the likelihood that these anguished words and images will resonate with aspects of the experience of the pray-er.

As Psalm 102 demonstrates, a highly individual experience of pain and isolation can parallel a similar experience of a group or nation. The petitioner in Psalm 102 places a communal request for the restoration of Zion (vv. 12–22) and the release of captives or exiles (v. 20) in the midst of an honest expression of individual anguish (vv. 2–11, 23–24). This royal-like function of seeing one's individual well-being merging with that of the nation exemplifies the picture of the human person typical in the Psalter (e.g., Ps 8) and the Old Testament (Gen 1:26–28) in which humans are celebrated as stewards or rulers of creation. The upshot of this royal image of humans is that each member of the community is called to take responsibility for sustaining the fabric of the community. In other words, each individual within the particular circumstances in which she or he lives is expected to see how awareness of collective responsibility has an impact on the common life: that is, the people's communion with God and one another. Here the interplay between conflict and communion is a tensive one in which conflict should have the positive function of promoting harmony and growth. Thus, at the conclusion of Psalm 139, the psalmist voices the request: "examine me, God, and know my heart; test me and know my anxious thoughts" (v. 23). This tensive inter-action between God and the pray-er is essential to the journey toward God. The logic of such tensive interaction resembles that of the hunter's bow: the pressure on the string must pull in opposite directions until the appropriate level of tautness is reached. Similarly, unless the entire embodied person undergoes the process of turning to God, there will be no harmony or peace for the individual, community, or cosmos. As Psalm 22 shows, the experience of the individual overflowing with joy and desiring that all people share in this joy typically comes only after some form of dying to self.

HOW THE PSALMS TEACH US TO KEEP EVIL IN PERSPECTIVE

Some of the pains we experience are inflicted by others. In Psalm 13:2, the petitioner complains about the daily "sorrow" carried within her or his "heart." The petitioner continues this complaint with the cry: "How long shall my enemy be overbearing toward me?" This concern about an enemy capital-izing on one's misfortune is reiterated in verse 4, which shows that the social pain associated with the loss of status is often more intense than physical pain. The identification of an enemy as the cause of one's trouble carries with it the danger of denying one's own responsibility. Yet the psalms of individual com-plaint readily acknowledge the reality of social evil and give a victim the kind of language that is needed to navigate through the confusion in which one finds oneself. In some cases of physical illness and social ostracism, the petitioner names the Lord as the one who has brought about this trouble (Pss 39:10; 102:10). An important objective of the petitioner's questioning is to be honest with God and to try to understand what God is expecting.

In Psalm 7, one who is falsely accused petitions God to intervene to set things right. He refers to God as "the one who tests hearts and insides" (Ps 7:9; cf. Jer 6:27). This description of God as one who puts us to the test is illustrated in Jeremiah's confessions (11:18—12:6; 15:10–12, 15–21; 17:9–10, 14–18; 18:19–23; 20:7–12, 14–18). In Jeremiah's extreme distress, he reluc-tantly comes to the realization that his own suffering is a result more of com-munal sins than of individual faults (Jer 20:7–13). The Lord was making Jeremiah serve as an example of an individual whom the Lord accompanies through times of contradiction and alienation. This survival of a distressed, but protected individual would give hope to the community that it too could come to new life after a near-death experience. In his confusion and anguish, Jeremiah does not claim to be innocent, but he insists that what he suffers is not payback for his own sins. In the face of Jeremiah's resistance, the Lord keeps Jeremiah's feet to the fire by insisting that he "turn" to the Lord (Jer 15:19). Such conversion or turning is a movement of the heart: that is, what lies at the center of one's thinking and feeling. Such "turning" requires that the "I" step back and allow more room for the "we" (i.e., both God and other humans). Unless the Lord is present in this process of relinquishment and rebirth, there will be no genuine movement at the heart of communal relationships.

One insidious way that the arrogance of one's foes can bring one to the point of falling is by provoking one to feel envy at their success. In Psalm 73, the petitioner reflects on the experience of feeling that life is unfair and that the way of the wicked prospers. The petitioner notes how the temptation to give up on trying to be good was near: "When my heart was soured and my insides wounded, I was stupid and could not understand; I was like a brute beast before you" (vv. 21–22). Here the anger that seethes in the heart of the envious one does not flare up at a particular point but rather eats away at the vitality and sense of meaning of one's life. So the psalmist notes that one's capacity to think clearly and to see the bigger picture of life can shut down; one can become like a brute that reacts only according to the instinct to survive (73:22; cf. 49:12, 20). When God visited and illuminated the psalmist's understanding, a transformation happened (73:23). The psalmist's former anxieties about the prosperity of the rich appear to have become non-questions. Now the psalmist can focus upon God's presence and can proclaim that this divine accompaniment will be everlasting: "Though my flesh and my heart waste away, God is the rock of my heart, my portion forever" (v. 26).

The evils that the wicked directly or indirectly inflict on the community are not to be overlooked or whitewashed. The duplicity of the wicked can have an especially negative effect on the fabric of the community. In Psalm 28, the petitioner invokes the Lord and pleads: "Do not drag me off with wicked ones, with those who are evildoers, who speak peacefully with their neighbors but evil is in their hearts" (v. 3). This lack of honesty in our dealings with one another has the potential to turn into a pattern, one which the psalmist laments in Psalm 12 upon realizing that loyalty and fidelity have vanished from the community: "They each speak falsely to their neighbor, doing so with smooth lips and a double heart" (v. 2). This duplicity of the wicked can cloak their hostile intent: "Their speech is smoother than butter, but war is in their hearts; their words are softer than oil, but they are drawn swords" (Ps 55:21). These wicked ones can pose a threat because of their schemes. "They investigate evil things, thinking 'we have completed a well-devised plot'; the interior of the human heart is deep" (Ps 64:6). In Psalm 140, the psalmist asks God to provide protection "from those who devise evil things in the heart, who stir up fights every day" (v 2). The wicked delude themselves into thinking that their wicked ways will not be found out and hated (Ps 36:2). Their world is one in which "transgression whispers to the wicked within the heart; there is no dread of God before one's eyes" (36:1). Such wicked ones do not hesitate to act hostilely against the ill and the afflicted (cf. Ps 35:25). In Psalm 41, the desperate petitioner cries out: "When they come to see me, they utter lies in their heart; they store up wicked things in order to go out and utter them" (v. 6). But such duplicity has no place in the heart of the one who trusts in the Lord. In Psalm 66, a hymn of thanksgiving, the psalmist declares: "If I had perceived iniquity in my heart, the Lord would not have listened" (v. 18). The fact that the Lord listened and responded favorably to the psalmist's petition served as confirmation that indeed the psalmist did have the right intention and was not laboring under self-deception. The psalmist then is obliged to communicate this saving action to the worshipping assembly (Ps 40:10).

Duplicity and scheming is not surprising in the area of foreign relations. The surrounding nations band together to make war on Israel in Psalm 83. Their alliance making is described: "they deliberate with a single motive" (Ps 83:5). According to Psalm 74, the destroyers of Jerusalem in the sixth century BC "said in their hearts: Let us utterly crush them and burn all the shrines of God in the land!" (v. 8). The typical prophetic interpretation of the destruction of Jerusalem is that this event was a punishment from the Lord and not merely a military victory by the Babylonians. This model of interpreting history as a succession of events governed by the Lord is fundamental to the faith of the Psalter. The Lord, enthroned on high, observes all humans; "the one who shapes the hearts of each of them is the one who understands all their works" (Ps 33:15). This God of Israel intervened in the politics of Egypt in order to bring the Hebrews out from there. According to Psalm 105, God "changed the [Egyptians'] hearts to hate his people, to deal deceitfully with his servants" (v. 25). One instance of such divine manipulation of the thoughts and feelings of the Egyptians is the Lord's hardening of Pharaoh's heart (Exod 10:1, 20, 27; 11:10). Such sovereign power undergirds the exhortation of Psalm 62 in which the faithful are urged: "Trust him at all times, O people! Pour out your hearts before him; God is a refuge for us" (v. 8). This psalm proceeds to give a succinct statement of the theology of history dominant in the Old Testament: "One thing God has spoken and two I have heard: that power belongs to God and to you, Lord, love, and that you repay each one according to one's deeds" (62:11–12). Even though the Lord works through secondary causes to shape history, the Lord does so in constant awareness of what humans are thinking and feeling so as to intervene strategically in their hearts. When evil seems so strong that one thinks it could not come from the Lord as a corrective measure, the Psalter encourages the afflicted one to complain and petition the Lord rather than to attribute more independence to the power of evil.

WHY SUFFERING CAN HELP US GROW

The consequences of an attack by an enemy can be positive. In Psalm 119, the petitioner laments that "their hearts are unfeeling like fat" (v. 70a), but then goes on to state that "it was good for me to be humbled so that I might learn your statutes" (v. 71). Attacks from foes when one is most vulnerable can break one down, as the psalmist states in Psalm 69: "Scorn has broken my heart, and I am depressed; I eagerly awaited sympathy, but there was none; for comforters, but I found none" (v. 20). As destructive as scorn can be (cf. Ps 109:16), the resulting state of being "brokenhearted" may be an opportunity to put one's relationship with God in order. In Psalm 34, the one who has been rescued by the Lord thankfully proclaims such saving action to be characteristic of the Lord: "The LORD is close to the brokenhearted, and those whose spirit is crushed he saves" (v. 18). A similar conviction is expressed by the psalmist in Psalm 147: "[The LORD] heals the brokenhearted, bandages their wounds" (v. 3). There are times in which the state of being brokenhearted comes about not as a result of attacks by a foe but rather as a consequence of one's own sins. Then the anguish of feeling separated from God may move one to a change of heart. In Psalm 51, the psalmist states: "For you do not want a sacrificial offering; you would not be pleased with a burnt offering. My sacrificial offering, O God, is a broken spirit; a broken, contrite heart, O God, you will not regard lightly" (vv. 16–17). In this situation of being ready to listen to God, one has stepped away from a disobedience characteristic of the ancestors. In Psalm 95, the Lord notes: "For forty years I was disgusted with that generation; I said: 'they are a people of erring heart; they do not know my ways'" (v. 10). At times such disobedience in the desert arose from the ancestors' desire to test the Lord: "They tested God in their hearts by asking for the food they desired" (Ps 78:18). At other times, such disobedience was the consequence of their sins; the Lord says in Psalm 81: "But my people did not listen to my words; Israel did not submit to me. So I let them go away in their stubbornness of heart; they followed their own plans" (vv. 11–12). So it is not surprising that at times the psalmist will plead with the Lord: "Do not let my heart turn to an evil thing or get involved with wrongdoing" (Ps 141:4).

The psalmist comes to the realization that failure to honor God above all else leads to God's withdrawing, which manifests itself in the psalmist's confusion. To counter this human tendency to forgetfulness and rebellion, the psalmist petitions: "Incline my heart to your decrees and not to ill-gotten gain; avert my eyes from looking upon falsehood; through your ways give me life" (Ps 119:36–37). The psalmist repeatedly recognizes that the call to faithfulness is the fundamental challenge of life. In Psalm 62, the psalmist exhorts: "Do not rely on extortion; do not futilely count on robbery. Even if wealth should increase, do not set your heart upon it" (v. 10). The right track is voiced by the psalmist in Psalm 119: "I incline my heart to carry out your statutes, an everlasting reward" (v. 112). Repeatedly in Psalm 119, the psalmist notes how important it is to be undivided in one's devotion to the Lord: "With my whole heart I turn to you; do not let me turn aside from your commands" (v. 10; see also vv. 2, 34, 58, 69, 80, 145; 9:1). This standing before God and making the choice to prefer nothing to God accents how human agency plays a key role in the journey to God. This exercise of the human will brings together what one desires with what one believes to be real. The lengthy Psalm 119, as a psalm that celebrates the "Torah" or Law, emphasizes how important it is to act oneself into a world centered on the Lord. The laws and precepts that become the focus of the meditation in this psalm promote the fact that the relationship with the Lord cannot be nurtured simply by thought and reflection but also requires action.

HOW CAN I BE HAPPY IN THE HERE AND NOW?

The promise held out by the Psalter is sounded in the opening words of Psalm 1: "Happy is the one who…" This promise of a vital, meaningful life is expressed in the language of the Wisdom tradition; the revelatory quality of this promise is discerned within the stuff of life—the interactions of humans with humans, humans with nature, and humans with God. By reflection upon life, the psalmist sees God's fingerprints in nature and detects many of God's expectations in historical events. Thus, Psalm 112 declares: "Happy is the one who fears the LORD, who greatly enjoys his commands…. Such a one shall not fear bad news, but with a steady heart trusts in the LORD" (vv. 1, 7). However, the laws of the Torah are not simply natural laws; they are laws that have been revealed by God to the ancestors directly and indirectly in their historical experience. Psalm 119 promises at the outset: "Happy those whose way is blameless, who walk in the Torah of the LORD. Happy those who observe his decrees, who turn to the LORD with their whole heart" (vv. 1–2). The vitality promised in these verses builds upon the experience of wholeness expressed by the psalmist in thanksgiving for deliverance.

The intensity of the encounter with God in a rescue (e.g., Ps 30:11–12) could hardly be sustained for an extended period of time. The psalmist is also aware of human finitude and in Psalm 90 describes one's limitations and shortcomings as an experience of divine anger in which God is turning humans back into dust. Reflection on such toil and trouble is supposed to bring greater self-awareness. The psalmist requests of the Lord: "Teach us to number our days honestly, that we might obtain a wise heart" (90:12). This counterpoint to the promise of happiness through obedience to the Torah does not negate the promise, but it does raise the question of how and when such happiness might be realized. Is there an expectation that there is an invisible world that can be accessed in this life and will bring us happiness (see Ps 73:17, 23–28)? Or does this promise of happiness demand an afterlife in which joy exceeds the toil and trouble of this life? The hints of an enduring life apart from Sheol (i.e., existence in the grave) in Psalms 16:8–11, 49:17, and 73:17, 23–28 accent the redemption afforded by divine accompaniment. It is the encounter with God that gives one the conviction that the destiny intended by God for humans goes beyond the seventy or eighty years of earthly existence.

Tasting the goodness of God should give one a vitality that promotes steadfastness. In Psalm 13, the promise of deliverance communicated to the petitioner leads him to say: "But as for me I trust in your love. Let my heart rejoice in your deliverance! Let me sing to the LORD who has been good to me!" (vv. 5–6). In Psalm 4, the psalmist embraces the vitality that the Lord has offered: "You have put more joy in my heart than their abundant grain and wine" (v. 7). The impact of divine accompaniment increases markedly in Psalm 16 where the psalmist notes that "because the LORD is at my right hand, I shall never totter. Therefore my heart is glad, my inner self rejoices, even my body abides confidently" (vv. 8b–9). The mention of heart, inner self, and body in a single verse accents the belief that God's presence with a person brings about a sense of wholeness and vitality characteristic of happiness.

What happens, though, when God seems absent? In Psalm 44, the psalmist protests that the community has been faithful, yet trouble has descended upon them. He says: "Our hearts have not been disloyal, nor have our steps turned from your path" (v. 18). In Psalm 77, the petitioner gives voice to the anxious distress of the community: "At night, I recall within my heart my taunt-song; I brood, and my spirit searches: 'Will the Lord reject us forever? Will he never again be well-disposed?'" (vv. 6–7; cf. Ps 13:2). To remain faithful and appeal to God to act with God's typical help, the psalmist meditates on God's great saving actions in the past. Reciting such saving deeds is a way of praising God. The challenge for believers is to remain "steady" or "steadfast" (Pss 57:7; 108:1; 112:7). According to Psalm 57, such stability comes by praising God. So when faced with hostility, the psalmist says: "My heart is steady, God, my heart is steady. I will sing and chant praise" (57:7). But then the psalmist engages in self-exhortation: "Awake, O inner self; awake, lyre and harp! I will wake the dawn. I will thank you among the peoples, Lord; I will chant your praise among the nations" (vv. 8–9; cf. Ps 108:1–3). These psalms advise that we should praise God and be fervent in doing so when times are difficult and God seems absent. Pouring out one's heart in trust to God (Pss 62:8; 69:32) acknowledges one's deeply rooted dependence on God. It is the opposite response to that of the wicked who think in their hearts, "God will not attend to it; there is no God!" (Ps 10:4). The faithful one who trusts in the Lord is one who, according to Psalm 27, has an inner voice that urges one to turn to God: "Of you, my heart says: 'Seek him!' I seek your face, O LORD!" (v. 8). The one who has such a desire to be with God is one who does not fear enemies: "If an army should encamp against me, my heart would not fear; if a battle should arise against me, even then I would be confident" (27:3). How to bring one's body, inner self, and heart to focus upon

God, how to bring one's desires, feelings, and thoughts to prefer nothing to God—this focusing, incarnational dynamic is the goal of praying the psalms. This activity of speaking with God, especially with words of praise and thanksgiving, will bring us into right relationship with God and others.

How is it then that praying the psalms allows our hearts to expand so that we live out of the abundance of God's love rather than the scarcity of our ego-controlled worlds? In recent decades there has been a recovery of the power of the lament psalms, that is, complaints that fervently call upon God to change one's circumstances. These prayers give voice to our experience of brokenness and help us to be more compassionate to those around us. It seems paradoxical that once we can recognize our brokenness—how we lack wholeness—that we are then in a better position to reach out to others. By shifting more attention to our common bonds as humans and diminishing the attention we pay to standing alone, but well defended, we recognize the value of trust. If we humans can generate greater security by trusting in one another, then how much the more so can we do so by trusting in God. Trusting wholeheartedly in God is a starting point that can transform the individual and collective worlds in which we live. If the primary goal of praying a lament is to grow in trust in God, then the claims of the ego to express its hurts and to appeal for justice are recontextualized within the larger project of coming into communion with God. The laments can help us to regain a sense of human agency but do not do so at the expense of allowing the human ego to put God on trial. The human person is encouraged to give voice to one's anguish and to question what God is expecting, but the Psalter has a larger goal in mind than offering merely a therapeutic approach to pent-up frustrations. Rather the Psalter insists on the difference in status between God and humans and offers a way that we can appeal to our divine Parent and so come to a deeper form of communion with God and others.

CONCLUSION

The Psalter has a purpose which is a matter of life or death: whether or not we choose to allow the God of our ancestors to draw us into communion with him. The choice before us is a costly one. The level of relinquishment of the demands of the ego required in order to follow the commandments of this God may seem prohibitive. The poetry of the Psalter aims to assist us on the journey so that our experience might be open to receiving God's assistance. The opening of one's heart to God must deal with the demands of our appetites, emotions, and thoughts. The balancing of these forces cannot rest on an idea of God but require a personal encounter with God. The psalms repeatedly speak of such encounters in stereotypical ways, which indicate that all members of the community were expected to experience them. As

the psalms invite humans into dialogue with God, there is bound to be resistance from the rebellious parts of the human person that long for autonomy
and question the reality of God. The choice between the way of the wicked
and the way of the upright persists throughout the journey. While integrity of
heart may seem to be an illusion to one who has not tasted the goodness of
the Lord, the Psalter aims to assist the person who must shepherd unruly
desires, emotions, and thoughts in response to the Lord's promises, commands, and teachings.

Evil brings tension into the lives of individuals and communities. The
Psalter offers help in navigating through trying times. The confusion and anxiety generated by illness, hostile neighbors, and warring nations call for God's
involvement. Human solutions not only prove inadequate but they also distort one's understanding of the situation. The troubles brought by lying foes
are real, but the capacity of evildoers to forge their own pathway independently of the God who governs history is bound to fail. The Psalter aims to con-
vince those afflicted with envy of the wicked rich and those injured by lying
foes to trust in the Lord and seek him with all their heart. Such troubles call
upon the individuals within the community to wager their lives on God and
to trust that God's plan will bring them into right relationship with God and
others. The challenge of making fidelity to the Lord one's ultimate concern
is nothing less than laying down one's life through obedience to the Lord's
concrete, particular commands. Denial of the seriousness of this choice
results in duplicity that undermines the fabric of the community. If one
believes that the Lord is ruler of history, then damage inflicted by foreign
foes must be assessed as occurring under the Lord's watch. What then has the
Lord tried to tell us through these events?

Affliction can be a positive force if it leads to growth in the relationship
of the individual or community to the Lord. To have one's heart broken may
mean that one shares in a death-like experience, but the rising up from it with
the Lord's help can lead to the expansion of one's horizons. The humbled
heart moves in a bigger world than the hardened heart constricted by arrogance. The humbled heart recognizes that true power comes through the
Lord's presence: a form of divine accompaniment that allows one to operate
from the standpoint of abundance rather than of scarcity. Such abundance of
God's power and love as expressed in the thanksgiving of Psalm 22 allows one
to see the interconnectedness of all of creation and to praise the Creator who
resides on Zion. The sense of human agency is paradoxically strengthened by
relinquishing it in favor of obedience over autonomy. Those who trust in the
Lord are happy even in the midst of trials. The reality of the divine accompaniment draws them into the mystery of God's love and power.

On the earthly journey, thanksgiving can be followed by lament (see Ps
40). God can once again seem to be absent and we are left to cry out "how
long, O Lord?" This crying out is precisely the kind of response expected of

a faithful member of the community. The Psalter repeatedly enjoins us to intercede with God, to remember God's former gracious deeds, and to keep alive one's desire to be with God. Nurturing one's desire to be with God in good times as well as bad creates a steadfastness of spirit that can be a bulwark against fear. The reality of God's absence should alert us to how much we have taken God's presence for granted. Psalm 90 characterizes life as a long journey marked by toil and trouble, but it holds out the strong expectation that this will be a meaningful journey. Such a somber view of life is counterpointed by the more upbeat outlook of Psalm 12, which declares that those who fear the Lord are happy and live out of the abundance of God's love. The Psalter lies at the heart of the Old Testament because it draws us into communion with God and others; it helps us to participate in the mystery of God's love and power and does not pretend to solve our existential problems by ideas and doctrines.

QUESTIONS

1. How would your life be changed if you were confident that all of your needs were taken care of? How is it possible to live out of a sense of abundance when I know that I am vulnerable and will experience suffering and pain in unpredictable ways?

2. Think of a time when something very good happened to you and you ran to tell a friend the good news. Then think of a time when a friend has run to you with good news. How has this experience of rejoicing together strengthened your friendship? How has this experience of shared thanksgiving strengthened your awareness of God's presence in your life? What potential does this experience of shared thanksgiving have for helping you to realize how life itself is a gift?

3. Have you ever experienced a time in which life seemed extremely confusing or even absurd? If so, did it feel as if God had abandoned you? Why does God put us to the test? Do difficult times help or hinder spiritual growth?

4. Can you point to a time in which you have said to yourself, "it was good for me to be afflicted" (Ps 119:71)? If so, how is it that suffering can help one to have a more authentic relationship with God and others?

5. Have you experienced a sense of joy in praying the psalms? If God promises happiness to those who meditate on the psalms and the Scriptures, how might I embrace this promise?

BIBLIOGRAPHY

Brown, William P. *Seeing the Psalms: A Theology of Metaphor.* Louisville: Westminster John Knox, 2002.

Brueggemann, Walter. *Praying the Psalms: Engaging Scripture and the Life of the Spirit.* 2nd ed. Eugene, OR: Wipf & Stock, 2007.

Clifford, Richard. *Psalms.* 2 vols. Nashville: Abingdon, 2002–3.

Davidson, Robert. *The Vitality of Worship: A Commentary on the Book of Psalms.* Grand Rapids, MI: Eerdmans, 1998.

Mays, James Luther. *Psalms.* Interpretation: A Bible Commentary for Teaching and Preaching. Louisville: Westminster John Knox, 1994.

Miller, Patrick. *Interpreting the Psalms.* Philadelphia: Fortress Press, 1986.

Stuhlmueller, Carroll. *The Spirituality of the Psalms.* Collegeville, MN: Liturgical Press, 2002.

Chapter 9

WHY BLESS GOD?

Christopher Frechette, SJ

READ PSALMS 16, 103, 134

WHAT DOES IT MEAN TO "BLESS" GOD?

In numerous biblical and liturgical texts, humans bless God. Here are a few examples: "I bless the LORD who gives me counsel" (Ps 16:7). "Bless the LORD, O my soul; and all that is within me, bless his holy name" (Ps 103:1). "At all times bless the Lord God" (Tob 4:19). "We praise you, we bless you" (The Gloria, Roman Missal). What are we doing when we bless God? How might we explain it? A glance at the biblical and liturgical contexts in which it occurs makes clear that "blessing God" expresses respect and reverence in some way, but for many people it remains a vague concept.

Jewish liturgy since antiquity has developed an array of blessings that structure daily liturgy and are suited to various occasions. The blessing of God in these prayers is best characterized as praising God for what God does. For example, the blessing after meals begins: "Blessed art Thou, Lord our God, King of the Universe, who nourishes all the world by his goodness, in grace, in mercy, and in compassion." While recognizing God as the source of the things for which God is praised, Jewish blessings function liturgically to release those things for human enjoyment (Hoffman). The Christian Eucharist is thought to be modeled, in part, on such prayers of blessing, and indeed the prayers over the gifts in the Roman Missal include similar wording: "Blessed are you, Lord God of all creation, for through your goodness we have received the bread we offer you...." The Eucharistic Prayer is best characterized as a prayer of thanksgiving. Indeed, the word "Eucharist" means "thanksgiving." There is no doubt, then, that "to praise" and "to give thanks" capture important aspects of what "to bless" God means.

However, consideration of the biblical expression for "blessing" God in its ancient cultural context reveals another aspect of meaning. When people who are in a covenant relationship with God bless God, they commit themselves to that covenant relationship and at the same time anticipate that God recognizes them and loves them as covenant partners with God. This insight can shape how we imagine what we are doing when we bless God in a way that can help us to grow in our capacity to trust God. Biblical and liturgical texts can do more than tell us what to believe. They are also capable of helping us to meet God as we sort through the reality of life, with all the messiness and struggle that it might entail. The biblical and liturgical texts that the Church give us for prayer can help us to see our situations and ourselves in a new way, and this does not mean that we have to sidestep the difficult realities of life. When we pray with these texts, we allow ourselves to experience solidarity with the faithful, throughout the ages and in the present, who have encountered the loving and transforming presence of God in the midst of situations similar to ours. Strengthened by this solidarity, we can open ourselves to God in all honesty and so anticipate—or perhaps allow the community to anticipate for us—that God recognizes us and will respond to us with love.

BLESSING AS A FORMAL, RECIPROCAL RECOGNITION OF STATUS IN RELATIONSHIP

"To show reverence," "to praise," and "to thank" all capture something of the force of what we do when we "bless" God, but something important is lost in these translations. Translating any text produces at best an approximation of the meaning of the original, since in each language words constitute a unique system of interrelated meanings. Biblical commentaries and dictionaries are useful, in part, because they provide explanations of the nuances of meaning that no single translation, no matter how good it is, can convey. To grasp in a rich way what "blessing God" means, one must first recognize that much of the biblical terminology for describing both God and human behaviors directed to God draws upon ancient Near Eastern customs regulating interactions between rulers and their subjects. Comparable to the practices of their ancient neighbors, the Israelites in many traditions depicted their God as a king and themselves as his subjects. The story of the covenant established between God and the Israelites at Mt. Sinai is foundational for both Jews and Christians, and the stipulations of that covenant are stated in terms similar to that of treaties between more powerful kings and subordinate kings.

Modern readers, however, must recognize that such hierarchical relationships were not stylized with the impersonal character often associated with a modern bureaucratic hierarchy. In ancient Near Eastern cultures, including that of Israel, relations between subordinates and authorities, although obviously asymmetrical, were described in terms that are at once highly personal and reciprocal. For instance, ruler and subject could be considered father and son. Furthermore, subordinates professed their *love* for their superiors; in the contractual language of the ancient Near East, a declaration of "love" by either party implied sincere and loyal commitment imbued with filial affection. For their part, rulers declared to their subjects their benevolence and their capacity to ensure abundance and justice, especially for the most vulnerable of their societies.

The biblical descriptions of the Sinai covenant reflect such reciprocity. In the following exhortation of the Israelites by Moses as recorded in Deuteronomy, the terms "love" and "hate" are to be understood not simply as expressing emotions but primarily as commitment to covenant relationship and lack of that commitment, respectively (cf. Moran; Lapsley).

> It was because the LORD loved you and kept the oath that he swore to your ancestors, that the LORD has brought you out with a mighty hand, and redeemed you from the house of slavery, from the hand of Pharaoh king of Egypt. Know therefore that the LORD your God is God, the faithful God who maintains covenant loyalty with those who love him and keep his commandments, to a thousand generations, and who repays in their own person those who reject him. He does not delay but repays in their own person those who reject him. Therefore, observe diligently the commandment—the statutes, and the ordinances—that I am commanding you today. If you heed these ordinances, by diligently observing them, the LORD your God will maintain with you the covenant loyalty that he swore to your ancestors; he will love you, bless you, and multiply you; he will bless the fruit of your womb and the fruit of your ground, your grain and your wine and your oil, the increase of your cattle and the issue of your flock, in the land that he swore to your ancestors to give you. (Deut 7:8–13)

Just as the Lord has demonstrated faithfulness by freeing the Israelites from slavery in Egypt, they, in turn, are to commit themselves to expressing their love for the Lord by following the stipulations of the covenant, the first of which is to worship and obey the Lord and no other god. To fail to do so is to "hate" the Lord; it is in effect to cut themselves off from relationship with God and so to bring dire consequences upon themselves. God, too, commits to ongoing activity that expresses love: to provide and care for them in various ways. Such acts of provision are considered blessings, but these blessings are understood to occur as part of a relationship. Throughout the history described in the Bible, God and Israel continually recognize one another as partners in a favorable covenant relationship and commit to act accordingly. As we shall see, the biblical term for "to bless" captures not only the Lord's acts of provision for Israel, but also reciprocal recognition.

In biblical texts, context makes clear that what humans do when they bless God is not identical to what God does in blessing them. Yet, whether God blesses humans, or humans bless God, the verb for "to bless" is the same, both in biblical Hebrew (*brk*) and in the Greek (*eulogein*) into which it was translated during the biblical period. Does this verb express something common in both usages, and if so, what aspect of "blessing" might be enacted both by God and by humans? In answer to this question, we might be tempted to point to the fact that what humans do in blessing God is a response to what God has done: God's activity of blessing entails creating and giving life, health, progeny, and the means to sustain a harmonious life as a society; humans' blessing God entails giving thanks and praise to God for what God has done in these ways. While this explanation captures something of what blessing God entails, it does not capture an activity common to both God and humans.

In both biblical Hebrew and related Semitic languages, the verb that is commonly translated "to bless" can also mean "to greet," and it is this meaning that provides a key to the aspect of "blessing" that both God and humans enact toward each other. In the formalized setting in which a subordinate enters the presence of a ruler or deity in the biblical world, this verb expresses the salutation of each party by the other. Furthermore, such salutation is not accomplished by words alone. It can also include a reciprocal exchange of hand gestures. What must be emphasized here is the reciprocal character of how the salutation of a deity was imagined in the biblical world. We might tend to think of prayer as something we direct toward God, hoping for a response of some kind. The language of blessing in the biblical world, by contrast, anticipates God's response more concretely. This is not to say that such language was ever believed capable of forcing God to respond. The Bible clearly affirms God's absolute freedom. Rather, drawing upon the formal conventions governing interactions between rulers and subordinates, this language of blessing captures a belief that anticipates God's willingness to be responsive in covenant relationship. Allowing this kind of anticipation to shape our own imaginations provides a means of cultivating trust in God amid the struggles of life.

As an analogy from modern life to illuminate the dynamics at play in an exchange of salutations between humans and God in the biblical world, a military salute provides an apt point of comparison in three respects: (1) the salutation is reciprocated by two persons of unequal rank; (2) in saluting the other, each recognizes the status of the other in relationship to oneself; and (3) the salutation can be enacted with a hand gesture. Comparing the act of blessing to a military salute makes plain the reciprocal nature of the activity by which each of two parties of unequal status in the biblical world formally recognizes the status of the other in relationship to themselves. It also helps us to grasp that such formal salutation signals a commitment to behave accordingly. To salute one's superior officer in the military both expresses and shapes an attitude of obedience to the chain of command, which is a foundation of military life. Similarly, to bless a deity or human superior in the ancient world expressed and strengthened one's commitment to serve that superior faithfully by one's actions. At the same time, however, the analogy of the military salute misses an important aspect of blessing as formal salutation in the biblical world. In the modern military, the relationship between superior and subordinate is regarded as impersonal. By contrast, in the biblical world, one's relationship to one's deity or ruler was stylized as personal. Indeed, the language of the covenant relationship that God and the Israelites share is highly personalized, and so we should imagine the exchange of blessing as salutation/recognition between God and humans accordingly.

The reciprocal exchange of blessing between the people and God described in Psalm 134 is best understood as reflecting the sort of conventional exchange of salutation/recognition just described. This brief psalm reads:

> Come, bless the LORD, all you servants of the LORD,
> who stand by night in the house of the LORD!
> Lift up your hands to the holy place, and bless the LORD.
> May the LORD, maker of heaven and earth, bless you from Zion.

Scholars agree that this psalm represents a liturgy that took place at the Jerusalem temple, but they differ in identifying who the speakers were originally intended to be. One recent view takes the first two verses to be spoken by the whole congregation to a group of priests who serve in the temple, while the third verse is then spoken by those priests back to the congregation (Zenger). Interpreted this way, this psalm highlights the intermediary role of the priests in the liturgical action that it describes. They are to raise their hands and bless God on behalf of the people. Then, on behalf of God, they are to bless the people. Based on other biblical texts that describe the manner in which priests were to bless the people (cf. Lev 9:22), they would have raised their hands also in blessing them. In other words, the exchange of salutation/recognition between people and God occurs here, but it is mediated in both directions by the priests.

In the context of the biblical world, notions of blessing, salutation/recognition, praise, and thanksgiving are closely related, and they express different aspects of what blessing God involves. When two parties bless each other, there is a reciprocal recognition of the relationship that exists between the two, each recognizing the status of the other in that relationship. For God and Israel to bless one another means firstly that each recognizes the status of the other as one's partner in a favorable covenant relationship, especially as it is memorialized in the traditions associated with Moses and Mt. Sinai. To recognize the other in this way necessarily entails both affirmation of the history of the relationship and commitment to fulfill one's covenant obligations to the other, anticipating that the other will do likewise. For God to bless the people affirms the favorable covenant relationship established in the past and expresses a commitment to provide life and the necessities of life. For the people to bless God expresses recognition of what God has done in the past and commitment to serve God faithfully by keeping the covenant. In this respect, it can be considered an act of praise and thanks. At the same time, when people bless God they affirm the existence of a reciprocal relationship with God in the present and anticipate that God continues in the present to recognize the people as covenant partners. Appreciating the reciprocal aspect of salutation and recognition central to the act of blessing in the biblical world can enhance our own understanding of what we do when we bless God.

WHAT BLESSING GOD CAN DO

Some reflection on how what we say in prayer can affect both ourselves and those with whom we pray will facilitate understanding how blessing God can help us to cultivate our trust in God. The words with which we pray express to God and to the people with whom we pray what we are thinking or feeling, but they can also do something else. Especially when we pray them together with others in a faith community where we feel at home, these words can shape how we understand ourselves in relationship to God (cf. Anderson). They can help us to come to terms with experiences that have the potential to disorient or overwhelm us. If our lives can be imagined as a journey of faith, then growing in our ability to trust God, to allow God to know and love us ever more deeply, is at the heart of that journey. For many of us, experiences that lead to feelings of fear, anxiety, pain, frustration, anger, and shame pose a challenge in this journey by inhibiting our ability to trust God. After such experiences, nagging questions—whether spoken or not—such as, "How could God allow such things, if God loves me?" and "Where is God now?" can dog us. However, stories, prayers, and other teachings from the Bible, as well as other liturgical texts, have the capacity to help us address difficult experiences by providing perspectives within which to comprehend what those experiences might mean for us as we go through them. Grasping how our own experiences, with all of their rough edges, are reflected in and addressed by these texts can help us allow the more vulnerable parts of ourselves to be open to them.

Psalm 27 begins, "The LORD is my light and my salvation; whom shall I fear?" It concludes, "Wait for the LORD; be strong, and let your heart take courage; wait for the LORD!" Here, "wait for" can also be translated "hope in." This psalm gives us words to acknowledge the reality that we experience as fear, and it helps us to accept that we need not deny or be ashamed of our fears. By the same token, it helps us to see that we need not let our fears imprison us. For, no matter what happens to us that might prompt feelings of fear, ultimately God is assuring us through this text that we can trust God to be with us and to love us. Perhaps the thing in life that we fear most is the loss of dignity and the related loss of a sense that we matter or have value to someone. This psalm and many other biblical and liturgical texts can help us to imagine how God gives us value and dignity that cannot be taken away. Still, for a variety of good reasons, to accept this truth in a deep way might be difficult for many of us at certain times. However, praying such texts with the faith community steadily over time can help us to be supported in solidarity with them. In this way, it can gradually open us to be touched more deeply by the healing grace of God so that we can experience more profoundly God's love for us, a love that gives us a dignity that no one can take away.

Biblical language can be strange to us, but this very strangeness can benefit us. Sometimes grasping the worldview in which this language makes sense has the effect of challenging perspectives that may be deeply ingrained in our worldview but run contrary to the heart of our faith. Humans are ordinarily inclined to self-preservation, and the Bible depicts God as favorably responsive to material human needs. At the same time, however, it affirms that neither God's fidelity to people nor their fidelity to God can be assessed simply on the basis of whether those needs are met. If we limit our understanding of "blessing" to God's giving us good things and to our giving praise and thanks to God for them, we run the risk of perceiving our interaction with God as somehow an impersonal exchange in which the goods given are central. If the goods become central, then when they are absent, it becomes more difficult to imagine how God can be present. Furthermore, in societies plagued by consumerism, such an understanding can unintentionally support a perception that the very purpose of interacting with God is essentially to obtain good things.

Retrieving from the biblical worldview an understanding that blessing involves reciprocal salutation and recognition frames our interactions with God as fundamentally personal and reciprocal. It invites us to imagine that in our very act of recognizing who God is for us, God reciprocates the recognition. As we affirm our love for God and our commitment to honor and serve God, we are encouraged to trust that God affirms our dignity and is committed to loving us. Of course this is not to say that God only recognizes us if we recognize God—rather, it is to appropriate the fundamentally reciprocal and personal way in which the covenant relationship between God and God's people is imagined in the Bible. It is to exclude the idea that our action of blessing God occurs in isolation from God's recognizing us, affirming our dignity. In this way it helps us to grasp God's commitment to love us.

Distinguishing this sort of recognition from a notion of blessing as thanksgiving for what God has done has a practical benefit. In situations in which the good things of life seem overshadowed by experiences of suffering, loss, or trauma, it is more readily comprehensible to understand blessing as reciprocal recognition than God's material provision and our thanksgiving for such good things. Seeing blessing as reciprocal recognition shifts the focus from what God has done for us to something more fundamental: the fact of God's presence with us and the love with which God sees us. If we regard the journey of faith as a process of learning to trust God, then to understand "blessing God" in the way that this activity was imagined in the biblical world can provide support for that journey, for it provides us with a way to imagine God as responsive to us and recognizing our value, no matter what. When life presents us with struggles, we bless God not in order to ignore them but rather to acknowledge them while confronting the common tendency to withdraw from God under their weight. Taking the biblical psalms as a model for bringing before God our whole experience, we can bless God and even praise God while at the same time expressing to God our frustration, anger, sadness, and fear. Even in the midst of struggles, in blessing God we have a means of confronting our tendency to conclude that our struggles mean that God has abandoned us or that our dignity is somehow diminished.

Of course, during such difficult moments, our hearts may resist the very idea of blessing God; doing so can even seem impossible. Especially at such times as these, solidarity with the faith community is critical. But a rich sense of solidarity, one that can support us well during great difficulty, is best developed over the course of one's life rather than left only to moments of crisis. Blessing God in a way that affirms God's responsive presence even as events may suggest divine absence provides us as a community with a means to embrace this paradox. Experiences of suffering can prompt in us a sense of shame, of lacking dignity, or being unacceptable in a radical way; these feelings, in turn, can lead to a sense of isolation from people and from God. It is at times when people ask, "Where is God?" that they need to feel solidarity with the faith community that respects their experience. The biblical traditions help us to cultivate such solidarity by providing us with ways of praying that allow for the honest expression of frustration, anger, fear, sadness, and at the same time affirm God's responsive, loving presence. The ability to navigate such paradox cannot be expected to develop all at once. By the practice of blessing God throughout our lives, through the ordinary ups and downs of life, we learn to open our hearts, even when they ache, to recognize the loving presence of God. The habit of blessing God as a community facilitates our receptivity to being moved by God's grace so that we experience a deepening sense that God sees us, recognizes us, values us, and loves us, even during harsh experiences. Praying with others, especially in liturgy, can cultivate in us this solidarity and with it, the ability to allow our vulnerability and our experiences of disorientation to be held before God. In this way, even during those times when we may find it difficult to bless God, we can feel supported by our solidarity with the community that blesses God every day, and in this solidarity find an opening to receive God's loving recognition.

QUESTIONS

1. Does it make any difference to you to understand blessing God as the human side of a reciprocal recognition between God and those who pray? Please explain.

2. How does the present discussion of "blessing" God resonate with your own experience of prayer, both private and liturgical?

3. How does it affect you to be part of a faith community that continually blesses God?

4. Read Psalm 103 slowly with the present explanation of "blessing" in mind. What comes to mind?

BIBLIOGRAPHY

Anderson, Gary A. "Anthropological Reflections on the World of the Emotions." In *A Time to Mourn, a Time to Dance: The Expression of Grief and Joy in Israelite Religion*, 3–9. University Park, PA: Pennsylvania State University Press, 1991.

Frechette, Christopher. "Blessing 1: Ancient Near East." In *The Encyclopedia of the Bible and Its Reception*, edited by H.-J. Klauck et al., 4:130–33. Berlin: De Gruyter, 2012.

Hoffman, Lawrence A. "Rabbinic *Berakhah* and Jewish Spirituality." In *Asking and Thanking*, edited by C. Duquoc and C. Floristan, 18–30. Concilium 1990/3. London: SCM, 1990.

Lapsley, Jacqueline E. "Feeling Our Way: Love for God in Deuteronomy." *Catholic Biblical Quarterly* 65 (2003): 350–69.

Levenson, Jon D. *Creation and the Persistence of Evil: The Jewish Drama of Divine Omnipotence*. Princeton: Princeton University Press, 1994.

Moran, William. "Ancient Near Eastern Background of the Love of God in Deuteronomy." *Catholic Biblical Quarterly* 25 (1963): 77–87.

Nowell, Irene. "The Narrative Context of Blessing in the Old Testament." In *Blessing and Power*, edited by M. Collins and D. Power, 3–12. Edinburgh: T & T Clark, 1985.

Zenger, Erich. "Psalm 134." In Frank-Lothar Hossfeld and Erich Zenger, *Psalms 3: A Commentary on Psalms 101–150*, 484–90. Translated by Linda M. Maloney. Hermeneia. Minneapolis: Fortress Press, 2011.

Chapter 10

WHY READ THE BOOK OF PROVERBS?

Thomas P. McCreesh, OP

READ PROVERBS 4–10, 19, 31

INTRODUCTION

I was first introduced to the Book of Proverbs in a university graduate course reading the text in Greek and Hebrew. Not the easiest way to be introduced, and no lasting impression was made. I moved on to other books of the Bible to complete my graduate studies program. That is, until my director asked me to focus on aspects of biblical poetry, as manifested in Proverbs, for my doctoral dissertation. I was back to reading Proverbs. This time, however, the book slowly began to interest me, then fascinate me, and finally challenge me. After all, how can a book that describes the lazy person as follows be all that boring?

> As a door turns on its hinges
> so does a lazy person in bed. (26:14)

The book has all kinds of advice, as in this saying, for example, directed to those who have not yet had their coffee in the morning but who must confront those who have:

> Whoever blesses a neighbor with a loud voice,
> rising early in the morning,
> will be counted as cursing! (27:14)

There was even an implicit warning for graduate students tackling a subject like Proverbs:

> The legs of a disabled person hang limp;
>> so does a proverb in the mouth of a fool. (26:7)

So there is some funny stuff in the book! Is that all there is?!

One of the main themes in the book is the encouragement of the pursuit of wisdom. The book uses a surprising technique: personifying Wisdom as a woman who speaks directly to the reader of her divine origins and her importance for daily life. This portrait is matched by descriptions of deceptive women (see chapters 5 to 7) who serve as models of how not to seek wisdom! How do these figures serve the book's encouragement of wisdom? What do they have to do with the proverbs that follow? Is the description of personified wisdom related to the portrait of the wife that concludes the book in chapter 31? These questions began to intrigue me.

The proverbs themselves were fascinating, not just because they could be humorous, but because of the succinct and pointed way they could present truth. One might see a warning about meetings in this proverb:

> In all toil there is profit,
>> but mere talk leads only to poverty! (14:23)

An important issue in this book is the proper use of speech:

> The words of the wicked are a deadly ambush,
>> but the speech of the upright delivers them. (12:6)

And how beautifully the value of good deeds is expressed:

> Whoever is kind to the poor lends to the LORD,
>> and will be repaid in full. (19:17)

All kinds of topics appear, for example: poverty and wealth (e.g., 10:15; 11:28; 13:7–8, 11; 18:11: 22:7; 28:8), weights and measures (e.g., 11:1; 16:11; 20:10, 23), human psychology (e.g., 12:25; 13:12; 14:10, 13; 15:15, 30; 17:22; 18:14), as well as descriptions of rulers (e.g.,14:28, 35; 16:10, 12–15; 19:12; 20:2, 8, 26, 28; 21:1; 25:2–7; 29:4), the lazy (e.g., 19:15, 24; 21:25; 22:13; 24:30–34; 26:13–16), and drunkards (e.g., 20:1; 23:29–35). Each saying has its own particular perspective. They invite us to reflect again on things with which we are familiar, as well as things we may have ignored.

PLAN OF OUR APPROACH TO PROVERBS

How does one read Proverbs? The book has its difficulties, including the question of organization. Proverbs tends to juxtapose seemingly unrelated passages or themes with no clear links between them. The proverbs are simply listed, for instance, one after another. A grammatical, rhetorical, or thematic device might occasionally link a few of them. Nonetheless, there are some clues in the text about structure that need examination. The nature of the material requires some study as well. The book contains longer pieces of poetry in the first nine chapters, generally called instructions. The short proverbs fill up most of the rest of the book. The final two chapters, 30 and 31, return to longer pieces of poetry. What is the relationship between these parts, particularly between instruction and proverb?

To begin dealing with these questions we first need to explore what kind of organization the book exhibits. The next step will be to explain the nature and purpose of the instruction, and examine selected examples. Finally, the characteristics of the proverb will be explored and some examples will be studied. The texts will be chosen for their themes of friendship and family in order to focus our research. A review of the poetry in chapters 30 and 31 will conclude our study. My hope is that this approach will help us appreciate the book and exemplify at least one way to plumb its teachings.

ORGANIZATION OF PROVERBS

As indicated above, an obvious division of the material is long poetry versus short proverbs. The first nine chapters, the long pieces of poetry or "instructions," generally describe wisdom or its opposite at length. Most of the proverbs, chapters 10 to 29, are two lines in length. The concluding poetry, chapters 30 and 31, replays earlier themes. Based on the nature of the material in the book, then, there are three major sections of Proverbs: the instructions (1–9), the proverbs (10–29), and the poems (30–31). Another simple layout is indicated by the book itself. A series of titles divides it into different sections although it is not clear if, or how, they are meant to be related to one another.

The book is presented as "The proverbs of Solomon, son of David, king of Israel" (1:1). This indicates the origin of the book's contents and claims Solomon's traditional authority as a source of wisdom (see 1 Kgs 4:29–34, based on the Greek text; or 5:9–14, based on the Hebrew). Chapters 1 to 9, then, provide background for interpreting the proverbs that follow, chapters 10 to 29. This second section is divided into smaller collections. The first collection (10:1—22:16) is also attributed to Solomon (10:1a) and the second (22:17—24:22) has "the words of the wise" (22:17). A short collection follows (24:23–34), described as "These also are sayings of the wise" (24:23a). The fourth collection (25:1—29:27) has "These are other proverbs of Solomon that the officials of King Hezekiah of Judah copied" (25:1). These attributions to Solomon, Hezekiah, and the Wise indicate these proverbs are worthy of being heeded. The titles also hint at a long history of collecting and editing behind the book. The last two chapters also have titles. Chapter 30 is introduced as "The words of Agur son of Jakeh. An oracle," and chapter 31 as "The words of King Lemuel. An oracle that his mother taught him." These attributions refer to non-Israelites, but the content of their "words" is traditional. All the collections draw on the older, inherited Wisdom teachings of Israel, both in content and genre. Consequently, the Book of Proverbs is presented as a "collection of collections."

THE INSTRUCTION

The Instructions (about ten, as estimated by modern scholarship, since the biblical text gives no indication) resemble some ancient Mesopotamian and Egyptian texts. They are poetic discourses composed of commands and prohibitions reinforced by motivation, encouragement, or admonition. Exhortative by nature, they employ graphic examples and vivid language. Delivered by parents to the son, otherwise unidentified, the presumed setting is the home. Both parents are understood as teachers, though the father is usually the spokesperson (see 1:8; 6:20). Although the instructions are presented as family tradition (see 4:1–4), they actually focus on the need for wisdom and its value for negotiating difficulties and temptations in life. They aim more at persuasion than presentation of new ideas.

These discourses are, first of all, parental guidance for the journey of life. But Wisdom also speaks. First, she warns about what awaits those who do not heed her (1:20–33). She then gives in chapter 8 a full presentation of her gifts for all who follow her. Two journeys are being symbolized. The first journey is about searching for a spouse, setting up home and family, seeking a good life, while avoiding sexual promiscuity and temptations to a violent way of life. The second is about the quest for Wisdom's gifts. But since the first will not be accomplished successfully without the second, the two journeys are most often intertwined in the text. The emphasis is both on encouragement to persist in these quests despite all obstacles and on warning about difficulties and easier, though more fateful, goals. In effect, the book sets up a basic antithesis between Wisdom and Folly. Success in the journeys depends on how one chooses between them. Thus, at the end of this section, these two choices, which will dominate the book, are highlighted: wisdom and life, or folly and death!

CHAPTERS 1 TO 9

Let us look more closely at some texts. The father and mother describe a graphic scene illustrating the kind of temptation the son will face (1:8–19). "Sinners" invite the youth to join them in their gang (1:10–11, 14) and promise treasure and shared spoils (1:13–14). The gang's methods are detailed in full: "let us lie in wait for blood / ...ambush the innocent; / like Sheol let us swallow them alive...." (1:11–12). These words are not subtle or disguised. They summarize the gang's plans and disclose the evil intentions behind them. A warning is added: these sinners lie in wait for their own blood; they set a trap for their own lives (1:18).

One would not expect a gang to be so explicit about their evil designs! But this scene stresses the ambiguity of speech. Many appealing voices will promise money, power, companionship, and intimacy. The youth's choice will have dramatic consequences. Such men as these bandits are to be avoided because their words betray the truth and lead to willful and violent destruction and death. Theirs are voices opposed to Wisdom. The young person is being prepared to recognize such voices for what they are so that the right decision can be made. Only Wisdom's voice will lead in the right direction.

Wisdom appears next, acting like a woman scorned in love and issuing a vehement warning (1:20–33). Her message is addressed to all, both low and high. For those who disdain her counsel and refuse to heed, the coming disaster is portrayed as a sudden and destructive storm (1:27). As with the robbers in the parents' speech, those who fail to heed Wisdom will enjoy the fruits of their evil ways. Her final remark, however, promises security to those who do heed her (1:33). Heeding Wisdom, listening carefully with intelligence and prudence, is the central appeal. Apart from Wisdom and what she offers, no one can stand without harm to themselves and to those around them.

In chapter 2 the father enumerates the blessings to be found in wisdom. Among these are divinely conferred knowledge and understanding (2:5–6), divine protection (2:7–8), as well as important intellectual gifts (2:9–11). But there are dangers to be faced on the road to wisdom, particularly two types of people who would lead one astray from its path (2:12–19). The first type are the wicked who lead others from the right way by deceptive and perverse speech (2:12–15), exactly like the bandits described in the parents' first speech (1:8–19). The second type, introduced at this point, is represented by the deceptive woman (Clifford, 48), variously portrayed as a loose woman (2:16a; 5:3a; 7:5a); an adulteress (2:16b; 5:20b; 6:24b; 7:5b); another's or a neighbor's wife (6:24a, 26b, 29a); another woman (5:20a); a prostitute (6:26a; 7:10); or "[one] who forsakes the partner of her youth" (2:17a). The suggestion is of seductive, adulterous women whose "smooth words" draw victims to betrayal and ruin. As the benefits of seeking wisdom are elaborated, the book also spells out in great detail the threats to the attainment of wisdom.

An important metaphor is involved here, that of courtship: seeking wisdom parallels the process of finding one's lifelong spouse (note the family motif):

Get wisdom; get insight: do not forget, nor turn away
    from the words of my mouth.
Do not forsake her, and she will keep you;
    love her, and she will guard you. (4:5–6)

As with the love between spouses, the pursuit of wisdom requires lifelong devotion. But one can also be led astray by a false love, sweet words offering empty promises:

For the lips of a loose woman drip honey,
    and her speech is smoother than oil;
but in the end she is bitter as wormwood,
    sharp as a two-edged sword.
Her feet go down to death;
    her steps follow the path to Sheol. (5:3–5)

On one level the metaphor describes the first journey, mentioned above: a youth seeking a lifelong spouse with whom to build a family. In the process, one can be too readily attracted by easy love, companionship, and pleasure. But the warning also alludes to the search for wisdom, the second journey. Here the difficulties of attaining wisdom, the discipline involved, and the time needed may lead one to be seduced by ready answers and promises of great rewards with little effort. All these will lead away from wisdom and life. The stark image of the deceptive woman functions as a warning about the serious issues at stake in the journey of life and the journey toward wisdom. One especially descriptive example occurs in chapter 7.

Similar to what the father and mother did in chapter 1, a temptress, "decked out like a prostitute," is described at length. She is restless, constantly seeking a partner for her lovemaking (7:10–12). The youth whom she meets has already been stealthily approaching (7:7–9). She is active and loquacious; he is silent, submissive. The scene is sketched in a masterful way: rich, perfumed bed linens; festive food from the sacrifice; furtive passion in the husband's absence; images of hunted animals; all taking place against the darkness of night and the threat of Sheol (Clifford, 84–85). The young man in this story will lose his life. The woman poses a danger as real as the bandits' offer. Association with her means submission to wayward passions, the loss of control of one's life, the breakup of a marriage and home, vengeance by the spurned spouse, and possibly death. Her deceptive and smooth words lead away from a wise, prudent, and prosperous life and put one on the path to destruction and ruin.

The woman, "decked out like a prostitute," is a foil for Wisdom (Clifford, 84). Just as this deceiver represents temptations to be resisted, Wisdom, in chapter 8, presents herself as the one who can provide all that is necessary for life. She describes her "divine" pedigree and enumerates all her favors and benefits. She appeals to all and promises prudence and skill for rulers (8:12–16), the moral gifts of justice and right, along with wealth and honor (8:17–21). She attributes her power and authority to her unique position at the side of the Lord during the creation (8:22–31). Wisdom knows the mind of the creator, understands how the world works, and can bestow the wisdom and knowledge required for living righteously and well. But one must desire her gifts more than anything else (8:32–36).

In the next chapter the deceptive, seductive women and their male counterparts, the malicious bandits from chapter 1, are summed up in the figure of Folly. She appears with Wisdom, and they both extend invitations to their banquets. Folly has done nothing to prepare for her guests but works to lure the unsuspecting and untaught into her traps, which lead to ruin and death (9:13–18). Wisdom, on the other hand, has set up her substantial house ("seven pillars"); prepared the meat, wine, and table; and sent out invitations by her servants (9:1–6). The banquet symbolizes the gifts that each can offer and the need to choose between them. How can Wisdom be found, and Folly avoided? What are the values and benefits for which Wisdom should be pursued? What are the traps by which Folly attempts to trick us? At the end of this section of Proverbs, therefore, we are left with two figures, Wisdom and Folly, two opposing forces, whose antithesis is a leitmotif for the rest of the book. Whose home is preferable?

Chapter 9 concludes with a choice between wisdom and life or folly and death. A simple clear choice, but generally one not made in a single, dramatic moment. It is realized, most of the time, through hundreds of decisions made every day which lead us, by slow increments, in one direction or the other. Experience, knowledge, and discernment of realistic goals are part of the choosing. This brings us to the next section of the book, the proverbs, which begin in chapter 10. They reflect the many different kinds of daily situations that require us to make the right decision. The attainment of wisdom begins with these small, wise choices, and even mistakes, made in the ordinary moments of everyday life. The proverbs underscore the importance of these moments, the confusion, the conflicting claims, even the ambiguity. Wisdom is not easy to attain, nor is the wise choice always immediately clear.

THE PROVERB

What, then, is a proverb? A proverb is a brief statement of some truth expressed in a memorable and striking way. The most common form of the biblical proverb is the couplet, composed of two poetic lines which usually parallel each other. Structurally a proverb can take different forms, such as a comparison, "Better is a little with righteousness / than large income with injustice" (16:8); a question, "Do they not err that plan evil?" (14:22a); or, more often, a simple statement, "A fool's lips bring strife, / and a fool's mouth invites a flogging" (18:6). Various literary devices are used to make a point striking and memorable. Synecdoche refers to the whole by specifying a part. Deceitful speech is condemned just by mentioning the lips: "Lying lips are an abomination to the LORD" (12:22a). A careful listener is referred to by the ear: "a wise rebuke to a listening ear" (25:12b). Metonymy, a related device, substitutes one thing for another. The mouth, the lips or the tongue represent a person's speech, as in "The tongue of the righteous is choice silver" (10:20a). The eyes, nostrils, hand, foot, bones, and especially the heart are also used in this way. Hyperbole is used in 27:3 where "a fool's provocation" is considered heavier than stone or sand. Oxymoron brings together seemingly contradictory things, as in 25:15b, "and a soft tongue can break bones."

Imagery is an important aspect of a proverb's power and appeal. Righteousness is compared to a "tree of life" (11:30a). This tree is an ancient symbol representing life, nourishment, and healing, so the righteous person is the source of such for others. How this is the case is left to the imagination. Very striking images can make the point about spousal and family relationships. Wives can be a "crown" for the husband or disgrace him, like "rottenness in his bones" (12:4). How they disgrace or honor the spouse is not mentioned. Relations can be such that it is better to escape to "a desert land" (21:19) or to a corner under the roof (21:9 and 25:24) than live with a quarrelsome spouse. Within the family or among friends it is better to have a warm and loving atmosphere around "a dry morsel" than a feast with strife (17:1). In ways such as these the proverbs suggest truths rather than define them.

CHAPTERS 10 TO 29

Focusing now on proverbs related to the themes of friendship and family, let us first examine some dealing with friends. A very positive attitude is simply put: a friend is for life (17:17a). The very next colon goes on, "and kinsfolk are born to share adversity" (17:17b). Now the saying becomes ambiguous: are a "friend" and "kinsfolk" being compared or contrasted? The nature of the relationship could be the issue. A friend's loyalty is evident continuously (else the friendship would not last). The loyalty of kin is presumed and more evident in special moments of need. Alternatively, the similarity between "friend" and "kinsfolk" may be the point; both manifest fidelity and loyalty. The proverb allows for a certain breadth of understanding. Another proverb has a different view and distinguishes different degrees of friendship. There are those with whom one's friendship is shallow, but "a true friend sticks closer than one's nearest kin" (18:24b). Here friendship trumps blood. In times of need, as well, a neighbor is better than family at a distance (27:10). Just the same, "familiarity can breed contempt" (25:17).

What are the threats to friendship? Gossip for one (16:28b). This is expressed pointedly in 17:9. By "forgiving an affront" a friend is gained; by "dwelling on disputes" a friend is lost. Another way of expressing this is found in 10:12b: "love covers all offenses." Restraint is urged in the matter of revealing a neighbor's crimes and misdeeds. Shame falls on the one who brings a case to court too quickly, if the accusation is not upheld (25:8), or by revealing secrets from a private dispute (25:9–10). A last threat to friendship is poverty. Several sayings affirm the power of wealth to attract friends (14:20; 19:4, 6). But poverty drives people away. Relatives of the poor man hate him; friends abandon him (19:7). What about the statement in 17:17a: "a friend loves at all times"? A contradiction? It is at least a reminder that the truths in these sayings are not meant to be absolute.

The next topic is family relationships. This presents an issue that must be addressed: the portrayal of women in the Book of Proverbs. Many times it is demeaning and one-sided, as in the example used above, 12:4, where the woman is either a "crown" for her husband or "rottenness in his bones." Lacking here, and in many similar examples, is a description of the husband's value—or cost!—to the wife. Proverbs emerged from a patriarchal society where male authority dominated and male perspectives on all aspects of life were the rule. This means that, in terms of a modern appropriation of this text, a more balanced approach, with accommodations to the realities of modern life, where spouses share responsibilities and authority, has to be made. In the following analysis, therefore, when what is said of the woman/wife/mother can also be applied to the man/husband/father, the commentary will reflect this.

The foundation of the family is the spousal relationship. Consequently, finding the right spouse is important, as in 12:4a: a "good" spouse is a "crown" for the other. The crown is a public testimony to the good judgment involved and a sign of divine favor. In 18:22 the human choice of a spouse means finding something good; it is also the result of divine favor. In 19:14, the human and divine contributions are contrasted. "Home and wealth" are passed on as an inheritance from parents—as a legal obligation; but a "prudent" spouse is provided by the Lord—as a gift. In reality, the wife was often selected by the parents in such a society as that of ancient Israel (and in many modern societies as well). Is the proverb stressing the importance of choosing a good spouse, in contrast to securing a house and financial support; or is it posing a conflict between observing the norms of society (accepting a parent's choice of spouse) and heeding the choice of the Lord (recourse to the Lord in choosing a good wife)? And how, precisely, is the Lord involved in this choice (Murphy, 144)? The ambiguity does not provide immediate answers but suggests the need to ponder the questions posed by the proverb.

What about the spouse "who brings shame" (12:4b)? The image of "rottenness in the bones" suggests a hidden and corrosive effect on the relationship that will reveal itself only gradually. One needs to be cautious and prudent, not judging by appearances only, before making choices. In 11:22 a beautiful spouse who lacks "good sense" is compared to a bejeweled pig! Physical beauty without prudence and wisdom is incongruous. Several proverbs highlight the effect of constant criticism and scolding. Such carping, along with "a stupid child," are the twin causes of pain and "ruin" in a relationship (19:13). The nagging drives people apart —in one case "to the roof" (21:9; 25:24), in another to "a desert land" (21:19). The relentless and ruinous nature of such bickering is captured by the images of the "continual dripping of rain" (19:13b; 27:15) that cannot be stopped. In another saying the attempt to manage such a problem is like trying to control a stormwind (27:16a).

Another relationship, that of parent and child, also helps define the family. What the proverbs take note of is the satisfaction and joy parents take in the child who is wise and industrious (10:1a [=15:20a]; 23:24 and 29:3a) or the shame and sorrow he brings on them when he is foolish (10:1b, 5b; 15:20b; 17:21, 25; 19:13a; 28:7b; 29:3b). Honor and shame do act as deterrents and help the child grow to maturity; but what about the intrinsic value of the particular wisdom to which the child gives evidence? The book does not elaborate but simply encourages the pursuit of wisdom:

> Listen to your father who begot you,
>> do not despise your mother when she is old.
> Buy truth, and do not sell it;
>> buy wisdom, instruction, and understanding. (23:22–23)

Failure to get wisdom brings parents sorrow, grief, and bitterness (17:21, 25), even ruin (19:13a).

Proverbs is uncompromising with respect to disciplining children. One proverb gets the point across simply by juxtaposing two ideas, "a wise son" and a father's "discipline" (13:1a; English translations do not always capture this juxtaposition of ideas in Hebrew; see NRSV note on this proverb). Although we can begin to understand what the proverb is getting at, the two ideas, a child and discipline, are obviously not equivalent. The proverb teases us about the relationship. It could be that the child *needs* parental discipline, or the child's wisdom *is the result of* parental discipline, or the child *heeds* parental discipline, and so on. The proverb invites us to decide. Striking imagery indicates the nature of the discipline. The "rod and reproof" will yield up wisdom (29:15a). Fools, especially, need blows and beatings (19:29), just as do work animals (26:3)! Avoiding discipline is to hate the child; the opposite is an expression of love (13:24). The image of death makes a dramatic and ironic point. Beating the child will not kill him, but will save him from a death due to undisciplined ways (23:13–14). It is important to note that these proverbs use imagery which should not be taken literally. For example, the last proverb's wisdom does not actually require beating children!

Possibly the best summary of family life from Proverbs is the following:

> Grandchildren are the crown of the aged,
>   and the glory of children is their parents. (17:6)

This saying points to the unique genius of each generation in a family, the respect and love that must exist between them, and the rich inheritance that one generation receives from the previous and bequeaths to the next. The proverbial text just suggests this with the words "crown" and "glory." In how many ways can we envision this to be true? When friends and the immediate community are also taken into consideration, we can see how Proverbs views all our human relationships as crucial for the structure of society as a whole. An individual's decisions can build up and strengthen these bonds of friendship, family, and society or weaken and destroy them. Wisdom is the only sure guide for the individual and society.

It should be clear enough now that Proverbs does not offer a coherently organized treatise. Rather, the sayings give varying views, now one aspect, now another, scattered at a distance from each other in these chapters. It is left to us to make sense of it all, to make connections. On the other hand, each proverb can stand on its own and be studied for its own wisdom, apart from the others. This much, at least, the book is at pains to do: to underscore the difficulty of the search for truth, to teach how to balance values and options in complex situations, and to encourage perseverance in the search for wisdom. The journey toward Wisdom cannot be accomplished otherwise.

CHAPTERS 30 AND 31

The last section of Proverbs, chapters 30 and 31, introduce longer pieces of poetry which, for the most part, repeat themes from earlier in the book. In chapter 30, the "words of Agur" reprise the theme of wisdom, but now in terms of the unsurpassable wisdom and power of God, contrasted with the limited knowledge and sinful behavior of human beings (30:1–9). Various sayings follow, including warnings about respect for parents (30:17), the heedless folly of the adulteress (30:20), and the dangers of folly (30:32–33). There are also numerical sayings which remind us of the limits of human wisdom, by noting what is still surprising, unexplainable, and mysterious in creation (30:15–16, 18–19, 21–31).

The last chapter opens with an earlier theme and completes the portrait of Wisdom. In chapter 1 father and mother addressed the child about the temptations ahead, and continued to give advice through the next seven chapters. That family scene is now transformed in this chapter into a royal one where a queen mother gives advice to her son about the particular temptations he will face (31:1–9). At first her advice about sexual impropriety and drunkenness may seem unfitting for such a serious occasion. But in a very clever speech the queen warns the king against succumbing to the perks of authority (Clifford, 270–71). The abuse of sex and alcohol make him both lose control and forget his obligation as king to protect the poor and the defenseless. He should open his mouth—not to drink!—but to uphold justice on behalf of the needy. That the poor should drink is understandable because of the need to forget their poverty! The poem hints at the power of the king's decisions and actions not only to weaken himself, but to weaken and destroy his people.

The book concludes with the portrait of a very capable wife and mother at home, about her work (31:10–31). She is no ordinary woman but orchestrates every activity in the house and around her for the benefit of all in her household. Her industriousness brings prosperity to her family, prominence to her husband, and goods for the community. She gives to the poor and provides "teaching of kindness." This portrait functions on two levels. On the one hand, she and the household she runs are the ideal goal for the young man setting out in life, from chapter 1, the way to which wisdom alone can lead. In one picture is summarized much of what the proverbs have been trying to suggest about wisdom's ability to bring life, good, and prosperity. This portrait also alludes to the well-built house and richly provided table to which Wisdom has invited all in chapter 9. In Wisdom's house, that is, in Wisdom's company, the disciple will finally realize all the blessings of knowledge, prudence, counsel, long-life, prosperity, and posterity promised in chapter 8. The disciple's "courtship" of Wisdom has finally become a life lived in union with her. So Proverbs ends by completing the journey begun with the parents and Wisdom in chapter 1.

CONCLUSION

Why read Proverbs? Because it poses questions, and exposes conundrums and ambiguities about life that are worth pondering. It offers numerous examples of human wisdom and experience that can be returned to many times for fresh insights. It also acknowledges the overarching wisdom that comes from God as the surest foundation for our lives. All kinds of threats to the pursuit of wisdom are suggested, yet the book is not dictatorial. The resolution of all the issues it presents is left to us as we search to embody Wisdom on our own life's journey. The Book of Proverbs can continue to give us much on which to reflect, but it will not give final, definitive answers or a complete program of instruction. The book is designed to make us think out these issues for ourselves with its guidance and suggestions, contradictions and ambiguities.

QUESTIONS

1. How would you define wisdom? Did you ever think of it as a goal in your life?

2. What goals in life are presented by Proverbs as worthy to pursue?

3. Is the feminine imagery for wisdom and folly appropriate or not?

4. Discuss some of the proverbs mentioned or referred to in the chapter.

5. What are your favorite proverbs? Why? Which ones do you dislike? Why?

6. How are wisdom and folly, and what each promises, made manifest in our lives?

BIBLIOGRAPHY

Boadt, Lawrence. *Introduction to Wisdom Literature, Proverbs*. Collegeville Bible Commentary 18. Collegeville, MN: Liturgical Press, 1986.

Brown, William P. *Character in Crisis: A Fresh Approach to the Wisdom Literature of the Old Testament*. Grand Rapids, MI: Eerdmans, 1996.

Clifford, Richard J. *Proverbs: A Commentary*. Old Testament Library. Louisville: Westminster John Knox, 1999.

Murphy, Roland E. *Wisdom Literature: Job, Proverbs, Ruth, Canticles, Ecclesiastes, Esther*. Forms of Old Testament Literature, vol. 13. Grand Rapids, MI: Eerdmans, 1981.

———. *Proverbs*. Word Biblical Commentary, vol. 22. Nashville: Thomas Nelson, 1998.

———. *The Tree of Life: An Exploration of Biblical Wisdom Literature*. 3rd ed. Grand Rapids, MI: Eerdmans, 2002.

Perdue, Leo G. *Proverbs*. Interpretation: A Bible Commentary for Teaching and Preaching. Louisville: Westminster John Knox, 2000.

Van Leeuwen, Raymond C. "The Book of Proverbs." In *Introduction to Wisdom Literature; Proverbs; Ecclesiastes; Song of Songs; Book of Wisdom; Sirach*, edited by Leander E. Keck and Richard J. Clifford, 17–264. New Interpreter's Bible, vol. 5. Nashville: Abingdon, 1997.

Zuck, Roy B., ed. *Learning from the Sages: Selected Studies on the Book of Proverbs*. Grand Rapids, MI: Baker Books, 1995.

Parts of the section dealing with the proverbs in chapters 10 to 29 were published in an earlier and shorter form that also included Sirach. They appeared in "Friends and Family in the Wisdom Literature." *The Bible Today* (May/June 2011): 149–55.

Chapter 11

WHY READ THE PROPHETS THROUGH THE LENS OF OUR WORLD?

Corrine L. Carvalho

READ AMOS 4–8; 1 KINGS 17–19; NAHUM 1–3

Anyone who has tried to teach prophetic texts knows the difficulties that these biblical books pose. The ideal audience is far removed socially and culturally from contemporary Americans. Audiences in the United States of the twenty-first century are generally baffled by claims of prophetic authority. The behavior exhibited by prophets in narrative texts is often viewed as aberrant in our culture. The language of the prophetic books assumes more historical and cultural knowledge than most casual readers of the Bible have. And even when the prophetic message is understood, many readers are often horrified by what the texts claim about God's interactions with the world. It is no wonder that many congregations avoid studying these texts.

When prophetic texts are studied in churches, there are some common moves made to mitigate the difficulties of reading them within their historical context. One paradigm is to read them in conjunction with New Testament texts, a move modeled by the lectionary. Many church-based classes study the prophets in terms of their promises for a new covenant, a restoration of a glorious reign of God, or the reparation of social injustices. Whether the prophets are read as precursors of Christ, moral lessons for a contemporary audience, or prophecies of end times, these approaches ignore the voice of the ones who cry out through the prophetic books, and "manage" the horrific images therein by either silencing them or projecting them onto some unrealized future.

This essay then has two concerns. The first is a practical one, namely that congregations should be offered an engagement with the text that is both true to its historical context and speaks to the question of what it means to be "church" today. What would it mean to take the prophets seriously in churches today? If one of the results of a community's active engagement with sacred texts is that the texts inform, and thus form, the moral imagination of that community, what kind of a community is formed by honest engagement with prophets like Amos, Elijah, and Nahum?

Secondly, it is impossible to understand the biblical books in their historical setting without fully understanding the consequences of poverty, disease, and war. I come to this issue as an historian, who also contends that contemporary resistance to the voices of the prophets mirrors a failure, whether through opposition or ignorance, to listen to the voices of those in today's world who also suffer from disease, defeat, and degradation. A community formed by this failure is one that ironically puts itself in the same position as the usual addressees of the ancient prophets.

READING CONTEMPORARY
BIBLE STUDIES ON THE PROPHETS

Most Catholic biblical scholars, of whom Larry Boadt remains among the best, have a keen concern to teach the text's historical meaning to lay audiences. Most introductions to the prophets do a fine job of locating them within their historical context. They talk about the historical situation of the prophet, and the challenges facing the Israelites at the time. They provide an outline of the individual books, and describe their major themes. Fr. Boadt's discussion of the prophets in his *Reading the Old Testament* remains a paradigm of how to bring the best of biblical scholarship into the classroom, and the Church is indebted to him for this work.

Historical approaches to the text provide a lens through which to understand the difficult language found in many prophetic books. I find that once audiences know about the history of Israel and the political decisions facing the leaders of the day, they can begin to understand some of the imagery of the material. They come to appreciate the artistry of the biblical authors and the variety of prophetic perspectives. But I have also been struck by how often those same audiences are glad to be done with the prophets, or at least with prophetic condemnations. I have come to realize that one factor that contributes to their uneasiness is the set of presumptions faith communities bring to the text.

Those presumptions are many. People presume that the God revealed in the text will offer no challenges to contemporary descriptions of the Christian God. They presume that every biblical text has a moral lesson that is easily applicable to an individual's life. People assume that the Bible has a universal meaning, and that this "universal meaning" is interchangeable with a single meaning. Therefore, whatever they conclude about the text must be what all other Christians conclude about the text. To illustrate that with a concrete example, the people in a women's Bible study that I led through the Books of Jeremiah and Ezekiel were upset when the view of God in the texts did not match what they confessed as the Christian God, when the lesson that they concluded the text was advocating was one they found reprehensible, or when their interpretation of a particular text was so troubling that they could not imagine how it could function for anyone as sacred literature.

While there is a growing body of literature concerning what have come to be termed "troubling texts," that scholarship either addresses a scholarly audience or it tends to be dismissive or hostile to the claims of ancient communities who read these texts as sacred. The people that I teach are often struggling to stay faithful in light of these texts. They need no help concluding why someone would reject them. But they lack the theological imagination to think of them as worthy of being deemed canon. They are also smart enough to be uncomfortable with apologetic approaches to these texts that attempt to "explain away" difficulties or with approaches that ignore what these texts say. I find that my students, whether they are eighteen or eighty, breathe a sigh of relief when I affirm that these texts really are shocking *and* that I read them as a believing Christian.

What follows are three attempts to apply a different paradigm to church-based study of the prophets. This approach parallels ancient Israel, which lived on the edge of poverty and social collapse, with modern communities in similar situations. I have used all three examples in my teaching. I have found students far more engaged with the biblical text when they understand that these texts contain legitimate questions about God in both the past and today.

AMOS, THE PROPHET OF OCCUPY WALL STREET

Introductions to the Book of Amos note that a major theme in the book is social justice. Amos had explicit economic concerns, a lens through which he viewed the rest of the world. For him, the stringent piety of the Israelites was tainted by their treatment of the poor. Several introductions add that this message remains important today, which it does. The problem is that these appeals to heed the social justice message of Amos feel like a simple academic exercise, rather than a poetic cry about the rippling effects of economic injustice.

When I was first introduced to the prophets, the notion that these texts contain a challenge to contemporary views of economics grabbed me no more than it does my students today. I could picture people walking on dirt roads to some open-air market to get their bit of grain weighed on scales, but that scene felt remarkably remote from my own life. Learning about the historical setting of the book can distance a contemporary audience from this ancient text. In addition, the rhetoric of an "all sinful Israel" further distanced me from identifying with those whom Amos addressed. Such distancing means that the book becomes a tool for thinking about something other than the subject of the text itself. In other words, Amos can be studied for its insight into Israelite history, its take on social stratification, its difference from other prophets, its use of visionary reports, and so on. But what picture of human existence does the book paint, and how should that picture affect the viewer? Where is the reader located in relationship to the text? Whose voices are heard through this text? If Amos speaks for the poor and economically oppressed of his day, what does the text reveal about the interconnection of economics, religion, and politics that challenge our own world?

Students of the Bible, whether in a college classroom or a church basement, are not disinterested in the effects of poverty in the modern world, but they seem to have difficulty connecting what they know about the standard of living among today's poor with oracles of biblical prophets like Amos. Often, when a connection is made, it is usually done at the end of a lesson on Amos; this is certainly true for the introductions to the prophets that I have surveyed, and, to be honest, it is how I teach the book in most settings. I spend about 95 percent of the time explaining the ancient world, which is largely inaccessible to the non-expert, and then about 5 percent suggesting connections to the modern world. But I have noticed more and more that it is this 5 percent that piques the most interest. As a result, I have begun giving that portion of the discussion more and more attention.

Biblical scholars have written insightfully about the need to articulate one's own lens when presenting a text. One reason to acknowledge one's own perspective is to allow this perspective to be challenged, softened, and broadened by engagement with other perspectives. One of the purposes of historical criticism is to show contemporary readers where their assumptions and conclusions do not match the ancient context. But introducing the perspective of other contemporary readers also opens people's eyes to the breadth of human experience that prophetic texts engage.

Let me give a specific example. In the book *Half the Sky: Turning Oppression into Opportunity for Women Worldwide*, Nick Kristof and Sheryl WuDunn interview women who had been sold into prostitution by family members because of the poverty that the family faced. Often these family members thought they were selling their daughters to work as maids or in other menial work. These families were easily deceived because of their economic vulnerability. The women talk about the violence that they encountered in forced prostitution: how they were drugged, beaten, and impregnated. Their stories are eerily alike.

I cannot read the Bible in the same way after reading these accounts. Amos 8:6 depicts the elite class (those who are wealthy in the ancient world) as those who "buy the destitute for silver and the poor for a pair of sandals." While this statement is a metaphor for the use of unjust weights, we also know from the slave laws in the Pentateuch that the notion of "buying" people who are in economic straits is more than metaphorical. Israelite men could sell their daughters into slavery in order to cover a debt. The slave laws in Exodus 21:7–11 make it clear that these girls were available to the men who bought them as sexual partners. To be sure, those laws do offer some protection to these ancient sexual slaves, but when these texts are read in tandem, the distance between Amos and today suddenly shrinks and the language of the prophet echoes across the centuries. The result of economic injustice was, and still is, tragic for girls.

I had a student once comment that female slavery in the ancient world wasn't so horrible because women expected to be treated badly. His reaction is similar to the way that the elite often react to newspaper stories of crime in their local community. Somehow that crime does not seem so tragic if the victim lived in a neighborhood with a high crime rate or engaged in activities like prostitution or selling drugs. Yet it is more often the poor who end up in these jobs, sometimes as the only conceivable option for them to escape poverty. Many students have never had the opportunity to hear the voices of women today whose lives match that of ancient women, women whose families live in such unrelenting poverty that their only hope for survival also carries almost sure risk of their being victims of violence. I suspect that when my students cannot hear the voices in the biblical text, they also do not hear the voices of people in similar situations today.

As an educator whose teaching takes place within faith-based institutions, I feel I have a role to play in turning up the volume for those voices. When I teach the prophets I have a unique opportunity to educate people, who are not evil, but who have been distanced from the reality of poverty often through the economic segregation that organizes so much of American society. This young student, who thought violence wasn't so bad if that is all one expects out of life, simply had not been challenged to hear the voice of the poor, even though he was quite familiar with the Bible. The same was true for older women I taught, many lifelong church-goers, all well-educated but who are still generally unaware of what it means to be forced into a situation where the elite are in a position to "buy the needy" for a price that only covers basic needs like shoes and food.

Few people who keep current on gender rights realize that slavery in the modern world is more rampant than it had been in the nineteenth cen-

tury. According to the Web site "Free the Slaves" (http://www.freetheslaves
.net/), the U.S. government estimates that 14,500–17,500 people are traf-
ficked in the United States every year; worldwide there are approximately
twenty-seven million slaves. In today's version of slavery, however, most
human trafficking involves women and children, as opposed to able-bodied
men. These women and children are enslaved to do menial labor as well as
to serve the sex trade worldwide.

Amos challenges modern Christian audiences in the United States to
think about the complex interplay of factors that allow such practices to
thrive. For example, the Book of Amos notes the role that natural resources
play in this complex system of oppression. To be sure, the book portrays
drought, famine, and blight (Amos 4) as instruments by which God punishes
sinful people. While contemporary audiences find Amos's theology of natural
disasters problematic, it remains a fact that natural disasters do not impact
the rich in the same way that they do the poor. Amos 4 depicts the rich as able
to ignore these disasters, to view them as insignificant. A quick glance at New
Orleans after Hurricane Katrina reveals the same phenomenon.

The way that Amos seems to critique all of Israel belies the fact that the
poor who were living on the economic edge are also Israelites. Amos is not
addressing an evil empire crushing a smaller country (we will turn to Nahum
for that), but rather that of a relatively small community that still fails to hear
the voices of their neighbors. According to the 2010 U.S. Census, over 15
percent of Americans, or 46.2 million people, live in poverty. The poverty
rate for immigrants is closer to 20 percent. Certainly these facts are not hidden to Americans. Populist movements like the Tea Party and Occupy Wall
Street all give vent to people's frustration with a system that seems stacked
against economic justice. Amos's diatribe against the elite on their beds of
ivory (Amos 6:4) suddenly sounds like an ancient version of the Occupy Wall
Street protests.

What Amos could not address, however, is how global economic colo-
nization contributes to families selling their daughters for silver. Ancient
Israel was not like the United States in its relationship to the world economy.
Israel, although independent when Amos was alive, was never going to control markets outside of its borders. Therefore the Book of Amos could focus
on the economic situation within the confines of that one small country. The
economic position of corporations in the United States is not the same. The
ways in which the use of overseas labor, stripping of natural resources, and
lack of reinvestment in local infrastructures contribute to systemic global
poverty is so complex, that when most of my audiences even consider them,
they feel hopeless. Did Amos's audiences feel the same frustration? If unjust
scales were a common practice, for example, could the actions of one person
make any difference? What kind of systemic change would Amos's oracles
have required? These questions show that the recalcitrance of the ancient

audience might have been similar to our own situation, where we see poverty but refuse to acknowledge our own complicity in the situation. The Book of Amos suggests that, at the least, it requires the involvement of the religious establishment, agribusiness, and the government. But at its heart the book recognizes that what is needed is a radical conversion on the part of a people as a whole to turn toward God and away from providing for the individual family and its posterity.

Reading the world through the Book of Amos makes the book come alive because the challenges that the book raises are ones that have not gone away. These are not academic issues from a world that is so different from ours that we study it like an exhibit in a museum. They are perennial problems for a people who confess belief in the God revealed in these texts. They challenge me to consider my role in an economy that inspires protests against big government and big business, that allows me the privilege to worry about natural disasters less than someone else in my community, and that contributes to a system where some families need to sell their daughters into slavery just to feed those left at home.

ELIJAH, THE PROPHET OF PYROTECHNICS

Imagine the following movie preview: "Against a backdrop of a clash of cultures so fierce that people are dying in staggering numbers, fire rains down from heaven! The dead come to life! See the hero chased across the desert in the wake of mass slaughter! Watch as he survives a near-death experience after being fed by an alien creature!" I asked my students whether they would be excited to see a movie that had all of these effects, and, of course, they would. When I asked them if they found reading the story of Elijah really exciting, they only laughed.

Why is it that modern readers don't hear the urgency in the biblical stories about Elijah? What role does the Christian educator have in helping students, adult and teen, see that, while these are stories of the past, they address issues faced by people worldwide today? People still die when they stand up against a political government that is unjust, especially when that injustice is carried out in the name of religion.

While I have always used the Elijah narratives as a way to get students to develop a picture in their heads about what a prophet looked like, I have tended to underplay the economic and cultural issues that serve as the backdrop of the text. While students are vaguely aware of the tragedy of drought in other countries, they do not know enough about it to understand the significance of what the biblical text tells them. Those narrative details, however, are an integral part of the story. In a narrative that tends to be sparse on detail, the explicit details about drought and starvation in the Elijah stories reveal that these are texts about the interplay of religion and politics, an interplay where the casualties include economically vulnerable women and children. The Elijah narratives commence with that lens in clear focus: a woman unable to feed her child because of the religious politics of the reigning government.

The statistics on women and children in situations of famine today are sobering. The Association for Women's Rights in Development traces the effect of the recent economic downturn and growing famine on women and children. It notes, by region, that as families have decreasing access to nutritious food, women are the first to cut back in order that men and children are fed. The organization Women's Leadership on Climate Justice notes that this disparity is exacerbated by environmental crisis. When the stories of Elijah are read in this light, it is clear how the severity of the drought is illustrated by the starvation of a woman and her child. The only male whose life is threatened by starvation, rather than by violence, is Elijah. It happens both times that he is in the wilderness as a political refugee. The marginalization of his status makes him as vulnerable as the women and children of the region.

The story of Elijah depicts a society where even the culture wars over religious values are played out on the bodies of the poor. A surface narrative describes political intrigue between rival claimants to Israel's throne where the "winners" get to establish a state religion. While these "winners" are primarily men, the depiction of the one woman (Jezebel) who stood to gain in this contest as unrelentingly evil reveals the fact that these narratives are about patriarchal power. Jezebel becomes the gaudily shod Imelda Marcos of the ancient world.

Casting the story as a "culture war," however, belittles the political violence that the stories highlight. The men who die in the story are engaged in a battle over religious dominance. Jezebel is killing the religious functionaries of Israel's religion and Elijah is battling the pagan prophets of Asherah and Baal, culminating in his slaughter of them all. This is not an American culture war played out in the media. It is the culture war of an Iran where the winners can imprison, torture, and kill the opponents. It is the culture war of contemporary Israel where orthodox Jewish men hurl insults at girls on their way to school. It is the culture war of Afghanistan where girls often cannot go to school, especially after the onset of menses, for lack of sanitation facilities during their periods and fear of rape on their way to school. It is the culture war of North Korea where grieving for a dead leader is a political act. Recent uprisings in Egypt, Libya, and Syria, where elements of religion, political power, and ruling families are intertwined, parallel Israel in the time of Elijah. First Kings 17 shows that the effects of drought are exacerbated by the government's channeling of resources into insuring proper ideology, and the cleansing of dissidents.

The pyrotechnics of the narrative that have become the focus for Western appropriations of the story are dazzling elements of the text. But are they the point of the story? Is not the main point that God is not aloof in these ideological battles? The author of 1 Kings is rather confident where God is located in the text, but the story reveals that the opponents were also sure that their gods cared about political power. Today, many people assume that their view of a political situation is also the side that God is on, but I think attention to the economic elements of these stories carry a warning against this stance. Although God may be on a side, when people start spending their resources to prove that they are right through religious pageantry and political persecution, then God is on the side of the innocent victims of such political maneuvering. Before the contest between religious functionaries in the story begins, God provides food to a starving, non-Israelite family. The "contest" between Elijah and the prophets of Baal is not over with the fire on the altar, but rather when the storm clouds come in off the sea providing a sustained source of food for the poor.

When Elijah stands at the mouth of the cave on Mt. Horeb in 1 Kings 19, he still expects to witness pyrotechnics. He cannot imagine divine power that is not packaged according to his preconceived notions of what that power looks like. Yahweh refuses to reinforce those assumptions. The revelation in silence or quiet attests that God's role in the passage is not primarily with that fire raining down from heaven. The quiet breaking of bread between mothers and sons is where God is most present.

Reading biblical texts in the context of a community of faith feeds the religious imagination of that community. The biblical narratives, by contributing to the religious imagination of a community, provide a narrative source for moral formation. Scripture study should explain the past, but it should also provide an opportunity to challenge naive ethical conclusions formed by those who do not understand the impact of religious and political decisions on people at risk of starvation and death. It challenges the assumption that God is best seen in glorious victory and suggests that God is more present among those whose lives are most affected by the decisions of those in power.

NAHUM: VENGEANCE FROM THE UNDERSIDE

Perhaps the most difficult texts for contemporary American audiences to understand are those that exalt God as a warrior who exacts vengeance on those who are "evil." On the one hand, the violent images that permeate the prophets are enough to shock modern audiences who have been sheltered from these images by a lectionary that often avoids them. When those texts celebrate military victories, the *idea* that God fights on "our" side is understandable, as long as that violence looks like the violence that meets communal approval: it is quick; it does not include torture; it is inflicted only on male

combatants who are not displayed as real people; it is controlled; it is justi-
fied; it entails "sacrifice" on the part of those inflicting the violence; it is
noble; there is no "collateral damage," that is, no women, children, or pets get
hurt; it has a resolution or end point after which the world is restored to
proper order.

Much of the violence in the prophets is far from this approved motif.
The depiction of the defeated city as a cooking pot contaminated with blood
and bones in Ezekiel 24 has no orderly resolution. Psalm 137's prayer to dash
the enemy's babies against the rocks does not sufficiently distinguish combat
ants from innocent sufferers. Nahum 3 depicts God throwing feces at the
defeated enemy, a less than noble act. Passages such as these raise problems
for contemporary readers who assume that the Bible provides images of God
that are "authorized" or literally true.

I have to admit that this topic is far more difficult for me to address,
since I too have the same visceral reaction to Nahum 3 as most of my students. I have the same reaction to the video that was broadcast after 9/11
depicting a crowd in the Middle East celebrating the fall of the Twin Towers
in New York. I have the same reaction to the photos of the sexual shaming
perpetrated on prisoners by U.S. soldiers at Abu Ghraib and, more recently,
the video showing U.S. soldiers urinating on three dead Taliban soldiers. Yet
similar images are found in the biblical prophets. Biblical scholar Julie
O'Brien suggests that simply repudiating such activities ignores the fact that
these acts must say something about human living.

In her book *The Lonely Soldier: The Private War of Women Serving in
Iraq*, Helen Benedict interviews women who speak honestly about their fantasies for vengeance. One young woman describes guarding military prisoners day after day who regularly demeaned her by shouting sexual insults,
threatening to rape her, masturbating in front of her, and so on. As one of the
only women in her troop, she knew that the threat of sexual assault from her
own fellow soldiers constantly surrounded her. Just this January, the
Pentagon noted that, while there were fewer than 3,200 reports of sexual
assault within the military per year, they estimate that the real number of
assaults was closer to nineteen thousand per year. Working within this envi-
ronment of constant danger and sexualized violence as a weapon of control,
she described how she began to fantasize about sexual violence in retaliation.
The interviews in this book demonstrate how a culture of violence and dehu-
manization within a system that was so recently primarily male-based and
patriarchal not only creates conditions where it was okay to kill an enemy, but
also where it was acceptable to kill children or rape your comrade.

Do violent fantasies of revenge play a significantly different role among
those who are not in power? My students often empathize with the desire for
vengeance found in accounts of the Holocaust. Hating the Nazis is acceptable, in part because they are experienced as a nameless group who perpe-

trated horrible acts on a defenceless people. The anger of Elie Wiesel's book, *Night*, does not present the same problem as the anger of a God who defeats the city of Nineveh. Is the fantasy of a people who have experienced unjust violence because of their national, racial, or ethnic identity at least understandable, if not commendable?

The Book of Nahum asks its audience to identify with a people (Israel) who are so hopeless that divine vengeance becomes an acceptable collective fantasy. I suggest that teachers of prophetic texts like Nahum challenge privileged American audiences to identify communities or individuals today who experience that same hopelessness. When the situation of the author is taken seriously, different aspects of the book's language come to the fore. For example, the violent images in Nahum are no different from the violence displayed on ancient Assyrian reliefs, at least in terms of content. But the two are markedly different in terms of the context of their artistry. The Assyrian reliefs represent the exaltation of a ruling monarch of a world superpower. As such the reliefs convey a battle that is controlled, orderly, systematic. The images seduce the viewer into not acknowledging the reality of the violence that they represent. This is the violence of the victor, an inevitable unfolding of a triumphant history.

The poems in Nahum, on the other hand, give voice to the experience of defeat from the perspective of the victim. Although the text purports to be about the destruction of an evil enemy, the language reflects a fantasized vengeance that wishes that the perpetrators of violence experience at least as much pain as they have inflicted. The chaotic flashes of images in the poems, with their sense of urgency and escalation evoke an emotional response in the audience, both in its original context and today. The fact that students of Nahum are bothered by the text reveals that this version of the images of warfare provides a perspective of horror missing in the exalting images from Assyria.

I find it fascinating that the Bible contains texts like Nahum that honestly depict these human emotions that our contemporary religion tends to silence. In the book, we have the voice of a people who have reached a point where violent vengeance becomes a collective fantasy. This book, it seems to me, requires that I cannot simply ignore the voice of people today who fantasize about vengeance. While I can reject the idea that Nahum justifies the acts at Abu Ghraib, I can simultaneously admit that sometimes injustice is so overwhelming that I must insist God cannot be indifferent.

I also have to admit that I have never been in that place. I have never experienced a hopeless situation where annihilation of the situation seemed the only solution. I have not experienced identity-based violence that threatened my group's existence or made me feel ashamed of my identity. I have not experienced daily threats of sexual violence or systemic messages that my identity was a "problem." But as a Christian, I also have to admit that this describes the situation of too many people in our world, both within these national borders and without. The Book of Nahum challenges American Christians to hear that voice, as uncomfortable as it may be.

CONCLUSION

I struggle with the fact that I feel that I am not doing enough to address the systemic sinfulness of the human world. I live in comfort and privilege, I have a stable income, and my children and grandchildren have never been threatened by starvation. But when I start wallowing in my own sinfulness, I remember that education is often subversive. While education can have the role of reinforcing social values, it can also challenge those values. Those of us who educate the privileged about the biblical prophets have a role to play in addressing the modern world. We can either help widen the distance between the ancient world and the contemporary audience, or we can hear the world through the voices of the prophets.

When teaching the biblical prophets, the goal of those of us trained in biblical scholarship is often to make that text better understood within its historical context. Because of the nature of the language of these texts, I am convinced that the texts are not fully understood without a sustained engagement with the economic, political, and social ills that they describe. My audiences don't understand those situations because they live in a social world that distances them from similar experiences in the modern world. Yet reading the prophets should bring into focus the effects of poverty, colonialism, and violence in both the ancient and modern worlds. When that happens, the language of the prophetic texts becomes urgent.

QUESTIONS

1. What theological issues might arise during times of national or communal crisis, such as famine, war, or hostile takeover?

2. Would the explanation for crisis be different among different groups in ancient Israel? How would priests explain the destruction of Jerusalem? How would women explain it? What about the poor? How would different groups today react to the same events?

3. How would the fall of a city, people, or nation affect the type of art and literature that would appeal to the survivors? How would it affect the way they told their own stories?

4. How might one's view of God be affected by crisis?

5. These texts assume God's direct involvement in human history, but this assumption may clash with contemporary beliefs. Consider the following

questions from your own perspective: Does God directly punish human sin? Are events in world history a result of collective sinfulness or righteousness?

BIBLIOGRAPHY

Benedict, Helen. *The Lonely Soldier: The Private War of Women Serving in Iraq*. Boston: Beacon Press, 2009.

Boadt, Lawrence. *Reading the Old Testament: An Introduction*. New York / Mahwah, NJ: Paulist Press, 1984.

Cook, Joan E. *Hear O Heavens and Listen O Earth: An Introduction to the Prophets*. Collegeville, MN: Liturgical Press, 2006.

Dempsey, Carol J. *The Prophets: A Liberation-Critical Reading*. Minneapolis: Fortress Press, 2000.

DeYoung, Curtiss Paul, et. al., eds. *The People's Companion to the Bible*. Minneapolis: Fortress Press, 2010.

Hutton, Rodney R. *Fortress Introduction to the Prophets*. Minneapolis: Fortress Press, 2004.

Kristof, Nicholas and Sheryl WuDunn. *Half the Sky: Turning Oppression into Opportunity for Women Worldwide*. New York: Vintage/Knopf, 2009. See also their Web site: http://www.halftheskymovement.org/.

Leclerc, Thomas L. *Introduction to the Prophets: Their Stories, Sayings, and Scrolls*. New York / Mahwah NJ: Paulist Press, 2007.

Miller, John W. *Meet the Prophets: A Beginner's Guide to the Books of the Biblical Prophets*. New York / Mahwah, NJ: Paulist Press, 1987.

Patte, Daniel, et. al., eds. *Global Bible Commentary*. Nashville: Abingdon Press, 2004.

Wiesel, Elie. *Night*. New York: Bantam Books, 1982.

INDEX OF NAMES

INDEX OF SCRIPTURE PASSAGES CITED

34:18	103	73:26	101
35:25	101	74:1	91
36:1	101	74:8	102
36:2	101	76:11	90
36:6	63	77:6–7	105
39:10	100	78:18	103
40	107	79:5	40
40:10	102	79:5–6	90
41:6	101–2	81:11–12	103
44:18	105	83:5	102
46:2	182	89:46	40
47:5	86	90	4, 97, 104
49:12	101	90/91:3	3
49:17	104	90:12	104
49:20	101	95:10	103
51	12	101:4	99
51:2–3	11	101:5	99
51:4–5	10–11	101:8	99
51:16–17	103	102	97, 99
53	59	102:2–11	99
55:21	101	102:4	99
57:7	105	102:10	100
57:8–9	105	102:12–22	99
62:8	102, 105	102:20	99
62:10	103	102:23–24	99
62:11–12	102	103	111, 119
64:6	101	103:1	111
66:18	102	103:13	67
68:5	67	104	6, 40
68:17	66	104:5–7	6
69:20	103	104:8	7
69:32	105	105:25	102
71:22	65	108:1	105
73	97, 101	108:1–3	105
73:17	104–5	109:16	103
73:21–22	101	112	97
73:22	101	112:1	104
73:23	101	112:7	104–5
73:23–28	104–5	119	103–4